# THE
# KEY
# TO
# GABRIEL

# By
# Coby
# Zvikler

Gabriel  Publications Ltd.

# A GABRIEL BOOK

*First Published in the UK 1999 by*

## GABRIEL PUBLICATIONS LTD.

Sycamore House,
Park Road, Colton,
Leeds, LS15 9AJ

**Edited by Heather Pedley**
**Final Edit by Celia Shalom and Annabel Evans**

**Black and White Illustrations by Coby Zvikler and Greg Smith.**

**Cover Illustration by David Coffey.**

Printed and Bound in Great Britain by The Bath Press, Bath.

ISBN Number :- 0 9535115 0 2

*This book gives non-specific, general advice and should not be relied on as a substitute for proper medical consultation. The author and publisher cannot accept responsibility for illness arising out of the failure to seek medical advice from a doctor.*

**For reasons of privacy, some of the names in this book may have been changed.**

# THE KEY
# TO
# GABRIEL

## by
## Coby Zvikler

PUBLISHED BY
GABRIEL PUBLICATIONS LTD.

**This Book is dedicated to
my mother and father**
*thank you for your love and support*

## *ACKNOWLEDGEMENTS*

I would like to give a special thank you to Heather Pedley, her help has been invaluable with the creation of this book.

I'd like to thank the guys at the office, Greg Smith, Karina Stanford and Linda Cruickshank for helping me get it together. Thank you to Maureen and Peter Shires for their support and generosity. Thanks to Celia Shalom and Annabel Evans for the hours of editing and David Coffey for the wonderful cover illustration. I would also like to thank my friend Leslie Kenton for her encouragement and support.

There have been many people over the past few years who have believed in me, helped me out and pestered me to develop my abilities further. I would like to especially thank my friend Costa Lambrias, who was around in the early days and urged me on. Thank you to all the Em-Power Research Coordinators who are devoted not only to helping others, but relay the necessary feedback we need to constantly improve and refine the Em-Power Therapy process. In particular Michael Brooking, Naheed Zaman, Rita Marr, Jim Marr, Wendy Hannon, Elizabetha Jovanovska and Rhona Magnay.

# CONTENTS

# Continued:

# FOREWORD BY LESLIE KENTON

## *THE KEY TO GABRIEL by Coby Zvikler*

Years of experimenting, soul-searching and just plain hard work lie behind Coby Zvikler's approach to healing. What he calls Em-Power Therapy has evolved out of it. This therapy is admirable, first because it does not impose any philosophical or religious set of beliefs on anyone using it nor does it place responsibility for healing in the hands of any but the person seeking it. Coby's therapy honours the inner wisdom of the individual soul. Finally, the whole purpose of Em-Power Therapy is to support what Coby calls an individual's Higher Self - helping him or her alleviate illness and pain as well as helping to expand awareness and realise one's highest potentials.

The Em-Power Disc, created by Coby, is a simple carrier of energetic information designed to enrich communication between one's conscious mind and the deepest levels of healing wisdom in the body. It helps make the link between the two so that the Higher Self can get on with the job of restoring and enhancing harmony, strength and well being. In the process, it helps strengthen an individual's autonomy and focuses a person's goals in working with it. How well it works for you mostly depends on how willing you are to work with it.

On a personal level, Coby is a sincere, intelligent and compassionate man with a wonderful sense of humour. He possesses a willingness ever to learn and to grow. He is honest and without a trace of the self-importance which so often comes in the wake of becoming a well-known and successful healer.

What he has created with this book is the beginning of what I expect to be an ever evolving, self-directed system for enhancing the quality of life, energy and joy. It has many blessings to bring to those of us in need of help.

I wish both Coby and this book Godspeed. They more than deserve it.

*Leslie Kenton*
*June 1998, London.*

# An Obsession With Time

*The sea beckons me to sail my boat,*
*to ride the waves of time,*
*as I ponder my existence*
*within the confines of my mind.*

*Beyond my imagination,*
*I will find the truth,*
*if I'm not blinded by the waves*
*upon the shore,*
*distracted by their relentless determination.*

*I will need a boat,*
*sturdy and fast,*
*To conquer the waves that never sleep.*
*If I take this journey,*
*I may never return*
*to the peaceful tranquillity*
*of my heavenly home.*

*Oh, but to ride the waves of time.*
*To feel the wind caressing my face and hair,*
*the warmth of the sun against my skin.*
*If I could only find the courage I need*
*to travel the tunnel of birth*
*and fight the gauntlet of my conditioning.*
*Would I be happy?*

*Is a transient existence*
*worth all this pain?*
*A life so brief.*
*Yet to feel love*
*for a fleeting moment,*
*all this I would endure.*

*My comrades are many,*
*but I know I am alone.*
*In this truth I can find comfort.*
*I'll take this step and live,*
*because truth is worth the pain of life,*
*and death.*

C.Z.

# PART I

## HOW IT ALL STARTED...

A ball of piercing blue-green light hovered over my cot. Dazzled by its brilliance, my eyes became locked into a gaze of fascination. An unusual warmth and sense of security enveloped my entire being. Smaller lights slowly manifested themselves, flickering and floating around this larger light. This is my earliest memory.

My father, a Polish refugee who fled the Nazis as a child during the Second World War, met my mother in Israel when she was on holiday there. They married relatively quickly and settled on a kibbutz about forty minutes outside the city of Haifa and I was born there in 1961.

Life on a kibbutz was very free and unencumbered, especially for children. In the 1960's many kibbutzim were agriculturally based. We had a relatively small community with a socialist ideology. As a small child, I was able to roam anywhere, knock on any door or play in any garden without fear for my safety or running the risk of being scolded by the neighbours. It was almost like having hundreds of aunts and uncles that you could visit at any time. Often I would go missing for hours on end, but my parents were never overly concerned because of the strong relationships within the community. I was always being looked after somewhere, by someone.

I loved being around all the animals and on most days my mother would find me playing near the cow shed. If I pestered hard enough, I could always get one of my 'uncles' to take me into the hatchery where I adored playing with all the newly born chicks. I loved the fluffy texture of their yellow feathers and I remember their hearts fluttering when I held them in my hands.

One day, my uncle had determined that I was old enough to understand the reality of a hatchery and so he showed me the 'sorting pen'. All chicks were examined when they were born and any that were sick were thrown onto a pile and left to die. I can remember, even at that young age, being horrified when I saw this. The idea of these little creatures being discarded and thrown away must have triggered something instinctive, so I stole one and hid it up my jumper.

I found a hiding place under a bush and looked at my chick. It felt lifeless in my hands and I thought it was dead. I felt powerless. Through my tears, I saw my blue-green light. At that precise moment a warm, comforting feeling engulfed me and I instinctively began to relax. I concentrated on this tiny fluffy body and in my mind and willed it to live. Normally, any kind of concentration at this level would have been impossible at such a young age, yet I felt so strongly for this chick that this emotion must have allowed me to instinctively focus my energy.

After a short while my hands became tingly, as if I had pins and needles in them, and the chick started to twitch. The more I thought about this feeling in my hands, the more the chick seemed to respond. A little later, the chick came back to life and I found a box for it to nest in and took it home to show my mom. I pleaded with her to let me keep it. She took a look at the chick, obviously must have thought that it was going to die within a matter of hours, and so said "yes". Anyway, my chick grew up to be healthy and strong. I suppose this was the start of my healing career.

I was about two and a half years old when this happened, and it is still quite clear in my mind. I would pick up any stray or sick animal or bird and take it home and take care of it. At this time I could only talk to my parents in very basic terms, but I'd point to the bright blue light that seemed to be around me all the time and ask them what it was. Obviously, looking back now, my mother and father were unable to see this light and they responded like most parents would by almost humouring me.

Given my age, they weren't particularly concerned and put it down to childlike imagination. I never had an imaginary friend, nor did the blue light ever actually speak to me in words I could understand, but it did make me feel like it was my guardian angel, that it was there to look after me and keep me out of harm's way. I could also see lights around other people and objects. The colours were varied in depth and intensity and I had no idea what they were. I suppose I just assumed that everybody else could see them too.

For family reasons we emigrated to England when I was four years old. My mother was born in Manchester, but spent her childhood in Wales. However, her family were established in the Manchester area and we came over to live with my grandparents in a small semi-detached house. We had a nice garden and the back looked over fields and marshes.

I remember the first time I wandered into a neighbour's house to play. A very large robust lady burst out of the kitchen and shouted in a language I didn't understand. I had never heard English properly - Hebrew was all I knew at the time and so I just sat there confused, with a blank look on my face. The neighbour went next door to fetch my mom, who came around to collect me, and the lady told my mother in no uncertain terms that I mustn't do it again. I can remember crying at this. I felt rejected; horrified in fact. I simply didn't understand why I wasn't allowed to visit next door and why this woman was so cross with me.

I had been born into a community with no restrictions, where everything was shared and we all looked after each other. I was now thrust into a life where people spoke in a language I didn't understand and became mad at me for no apparent reason and I was limited to the confines of one house and one garden. I had nothing to latch onto, no comparisons. As a four-year-old, the extreme contrast must have been a huge shock to my system.

Several months after our arrival in England, I started at my first primary school. I still didn't understand a word of English and on top of the recent restrictions I became even more traumatised. Whether out of mild shock or childlike protest, I actually stopped speaking altogether. Then an unusual thing happened. About two months later, I started speaking again but in perfect English! Even when my parents spoke to me in Hebrew I would answer in English. At school the other children had initially ridiculed the way I spoke and I think I must have put up some kind of emotional mental barrier, because I rejected the Hebrew language altogether. I could still understand it, but refused to speak it. And this emotional block is still with me today.

At school I was at best uncooperative, mostly disruptive, and I would often play truant. If I could get away with it, I'd much rather wander the corridors or sneak outside to play. Sometimes I could avoid detection for the best part of a day, but my frustrated and annoyed teachers would catch up with me sooner or later, reprimand me and make me attend class. I think I had more visits to the headmaster than anyone else in my year!

For some reason I was able to talk about most subjects even if I had missed the lessons. I now think that I was unconsciously reading the minds of the other children around me, or of my teachers perhaps. I remember being incredibly confused over my maths lessons because I would know the answer to virtually any maths problem put in front of me, almost immediately. I now believe that these answers came from an inner knowing or intuition, but at the time they just appeared in my mind. It was like I 'felt' them; I experienced them on some emotional level. Yet on many other emotional levels I was totally unable to feel anything at all.

My teachers became baffled. They couldn't understand how I had arrived at the answers so quickly and they constantly challenged me, believing me to be blatantly cheating in some way. Time and time again they would ask me how I had worked out the answer, but naturally I couldn't tell them because I didn't know. At this young age, I couldn't understand why the answer on its own wasn't good enough, and why I should be reprimanded for getting my maths right. So this led me to become quite withdrawn once again.

As I grew older, my academic work slid further downhill. This was so drastic that at the age of eleven it was concluded that I might have some kind of learning disability like dyslexia. A decision was taken to hold me back for a year, which meant that in my first year of high school I was a year older than all the other children. I was surrounded by younger kids who appeared to be as smart or smarter than I was and so my self-esteem took a dramatic nose-dive. It was at this point that I realised for myself that I was way behind everyone else my age, and I therefore became determined to succeed. On most of my school reports my teachers noted that I tried hard. My parents obviously wanted the best for me and supported me as much as they could by arranging extra tuition for me. Nevertheless, the general comments were that I lacked the ability to concentrate, even though it was obvious to those teaching me that I was making the effort.

My concentration actually came in waves. At certain times I was able to hear and focus quite easily on my work, but most of the time it felt like I was immersed in water.

When my teachers spoke to me I could see their mouths moving but could only hear muffled noises. At times like this, it felt like I was living in a fish tank. I was totally distracted; I couldn't concentrate because of the continual barrage of visual and sensory information I was receiving from all directions. I could feel little internal sensations, fluttering feelings in my stomach, that I now know to be energy shifting throughout my body.

My familiar bright blue light appeared sporadically but, depending on the mood of my teachers and friends, I would also see masses of colours around them too. These experiences were very overwhelming for me and I found it incredibly difficult to stay in control.

Sometimes it was as if I was almost in a hypnotic state. So I suppose it is no wonder that academic information floated past me and that I was unable to absorb it on a conscious level.

I tried every trick in the book to succeed at school, including using telepathic abilities to compensate for my learning problems. I would always sit next to the brainy kids and I found that my handwriting would change depending on who I was sitting next to. My exercise books looked as if several different people had been writing in them. It was as if I was picking up the mannerisms and idiosyncrasies of those around me. Obviously I didn't know or understand what was happening at the time and it is only on reflection that I can appreciate it and rationalise it.

I am a firm believer that all children possess these abilities and, if forced by circumstances beyond their control, they will use them to compensate for any learning difficulties they may have. Eventually, through determination, hard work and a lot of additional tuition, I managed to leave school with a basic education.

However, as a child, having unusual abilities did have its 'up' side too. I was always popular at parties when my friends would insist I perform my 'spooky tricks'. I found out at quite an early age that if I focused my attention on a friend's arm or leg I could get it to move on its own.

At parties, I would get my friends to gather in a circle and keep quiet while I stood in the centre and concentrated on one person at a time. Sure enough, as I focused on them I could get them to involuntarily move one or several limbs at once.

Sometimes I would get three or four volunteers to lie on the floor and I would concentrate on them all at the same time. All the others would fall about laughing, watching as their friends' legs and arms spontaneously jerked and moved. Eventually over time, if I concentrated hard enough, I could even get some of them to stand on their heads. When this happened, the lights in the room would flash on and off which would add to the spooky drama.

We would often play a series of mind reading games and also a game called 'Murder in the Dark'. One of the kids would volunteer to leave the room, the lights would be turned down until the room was pitch black, and the rest of us would crouch in corners or behind furniture in literally any hiding place we could find. The volunteer would then come back in and try to identify the rest of us, just by touch. They would always pick me out first time, because they said that my body gave off some kind of energy or they could feel a force field around me. As I was a constant loser at this game, I naturally hated it.

Throughout my teenage years, as my friends and family members developed their bad backs, suffered toothaches and various other aches and pains, I found that I was able to greatly relieve their pain and in many instances remove it for them completely.

My hands became a bit like an anaesthetic. It was a common occurrence for my friends to telephone or call round to ask me to perform this pain-relieving trick. It got to the point where those closest to me wouldn't even ask; they would just grab my hand and put it on their point of pain.

Every time my dad had a problem, like elbow strain or toothache, he would always ask me if I could fix it for him. I would put my hands where it hurt the most and within a couple of minutes he would be feeling all right again. Even to this day, he doesn't really understand exactly what happens and always puts it down to me having 'hot hands'.

In the seventies, when Uri Geller started bending spoons, I became interested in people with 'special powers'. At that time, I tried hard to bend spoons like Uri and I had a bit of success although I found it quite difficult. All the same, I practised and practised, much to my mom's horror. This short-lived career ended suddenly when she opened the cutlery drawer and discovered that all the spoons and forks were bent, some of them sideways. I thought that this was a brilliant achievement, but she didn't believe for one minute that I had done it just by thinking about it. She assumed that I must have just manually bent them and I got a serious telling off for it.

At this age, every time I used my concentration to do something unusual like fix a toothache or bend a spoon, or if I got frustrated or annoyed for any reason, 'things' started to happen: lights flashed, radios switched themselves on and off, or TV channels jumped.

These kinds of things became more and more frequent until it got to the point where they started to happen to me all the time. My parents would always try and explain away all these little events as flukes or coincidences, but there were so many of them that it all became a bit hard for everyone to believe.

I found out that if I stood under a light and used my concentration then I could make the light either dim or brighten. This was much easier if it was connected to a dimmer switch, but it made me feel really tired and a bit sick and I would have to sleep afterwards. However, most of the time the electrical mishaps seemed to happen for no apparent reason and became a common occurrence.

Since the age of five I had been able to fix things. In the late sixties, my dad was a travelling salesman specialising in electrical and fancy goods. Often he would get damaged or faulty returns and he would pass them on to me just to play with. At the age of seven, I could easily fix a radio or clock by just taking the back off it and mending it. I never knew how I did it, but the objects always seemed to work afterwards.

I also went through a phase where for no apparent reason I would take a spade and go and dig a hole. I would wander around until I found the right spot somewhere in our back garden or the park or playing field, and I would just dig. Within the space of two years I found two solid silver trays, a glass bowl, more than a hundred Roman and old English coins, various plates, watches, clocks and rings. A lot of it was useless junk, but some of it was quite rare and valuable and in those instances I would hand it in.

As a teenager, I would dream about where I could find stuff. I would see the place quite clearly in my dreams and my imaginary finds would always be valuable - of gold or precious jewels. In reality, I would more often than not just dig up junk, but nevertheless I would always find something at the place that I had dreamed about.

In the early eighties I became more seriously interested in parapsychology, ESP and personal development as I decided to channel my abilities towards doing something useful and beneficial. I read books from the library about people with 'special powers' and on alternative healing. While these books were interesting and descriptive, none of them told me how it was possible for people like me to develop their abilities further.

I started to realise that there were thousands of people around the world demonstrating a diversity of unusual and unique abilities, from mind reading to astral travel, spoon bending to predicting the future. But none of the books that I read at that time explained how they did it, or how they could teach others to do the same or help with their development.

I was looking for someone with advanced abilities to take me under their wing and help me. At this time, although I had a vivid imagination, I also had a very logical thinking process. Unfortunately none of the people I came across could ever consistently or successfully demonstrate the abilities that they claimed to have when challenged in a controlled environment.

Throughout this period of my life I met many psychic or religious eccentrics who claimed to be everything from Jesus reincarnated to aliens from another planet, but none of them could provide me with one shred of evidence or proof when I asked them to. This was one extreme of the type of person I came across in my personal investigation into the paranormal.

At the other extreme I met many who would attempt to explain away every single phenomenon as being some kind of conjurer's trick or a natural event. For example, if they could demonstrate how it was possible with sleight of hand to manually bend a spoon under the watchful eye of others, then that was how it was always done and anyone who claimed to do it with their minds must be cheating. It was as simple as that; there was no room for debate with these kinds of people. Because it was possible to hypnotise someone and get them to lift their arms up in a hypnotic trance, then they ascertained that that was what I did. The possibility that I was able to achieve this in a totally different way to hypnosis was not remotely open to them.

I also found that some people investigating the paranormal are extremely gullible and are prepared to believe almost anything, often being fooled by those cleverer than themselves. In contrast, many others, even when presented with irrefutable evidence that paranormal abilities and phenomena exist, dismiss them totally out of hand without proper investigation and analysis.

During this period, I was referred to three parapsychology students who wanted to investigate my personal claims. A couple of weeks later one of them called me to arrange a meeting in my local pub. I thought it was a bit of a strange meeting place as they were welcome to come to my home, but they said that they preferred to meet somewhere fairly public. I thought this was odd, but nevertheless left it at that.

After we had made our introductions they told me that, in their past experience of investigating the paranormal, more often than not people who claimed to have incredible abilities were usually either delusional or suffering from some kind of emotional disorder. I laughed at this, but I couldn't help but wonder what their impression of me was and felt inclined to ask them. They said that on the surface I appeared to be fairly rational although the claims that I made were bordering on the ridiculous! Anyway, they must have been sufficiently confident that I wasn't a lunatic because they came back with me to my house to conduct a couple of paranormal experiments.

Understandably I was very nervous at this point. I didn't know them, they claimed to be psychic investigators and now all their attention was directed at me. I stood behind one of them and put my hand about six inches above his head and asked him to tell me if he felt anything. After a few moments, he said that he felt prickly sensations on the crown of his head and shoulders and it was as if his hair was standing on end. I then sat opposite him and told him to put his hands in his lap and just sit comfortably and relaxed. I concentrated on his hands for about five minutes but nothing seemed to be happening. Then slowly his hands started to rise up spontaneously.

At this initial meeting they concluded that I did have some

kind of ability but that they couldn't define exactly what it was. It was obvious though, that they wanted to help me. I explained to them that I would like to develop more, to try and direct my abilities towards doing something useful or positive. At this time they were also investigating psychic healing and they suggested that I should look into this. The idea of healing appealed to me as it had both practical and positive applications so I took their advice. The following week I went with them to visit a healing group in Manchester.

The healing group took place in a shared student house. There were approximately fifteen 'new age' types there. I was really excited at the prospect of meeting up with people who all had a common interest and could teach me how to develop and use my abilities for something positive. I was impressed with their knowledge and explanations of what it was I had been experiencing throughout my entire life and I realised instantly just how much I had to learn and what a novice I was.

I spoke with a girl called Valerie who had been in an accident some years previously and had been told that she would never walk again. A gentleman called John Cain had healed her and she told me the story of her miraculous recovery. The accident had been horrific and her injuries had been very serious to the point where conventional medical doctors had just about given up on her. It had been determined that not only would she have to live out the rest of her life confined to a wheelchair but also that her life would be a short one. Valerie had slumped into a depression, but her parents had persuaded her to visit John Cain in Liverpool to see if his healing could help her. Her recovery, after Cain's treatments, had dumbfounded the medical profession. From what I could see, Valerie was completely healed of all her injuries.

This story inspired me tremendously. I found out later that Valerie had written a book about Cain who had in fact started healing quite late in his life after retiring from a successful business career. During his treatments patients would often go into altered states of consciousness as well as showing spontaneous physical movement and I couldn't help but notice some similarities between these stories and my own experiences.

Unfortunately Cain had recently died and so I was denied the chance of meeting him. It is true to say though that he left a legacy of healing and has trained many others in his methods.

Valerie's knowledge of the body's energy field and healing helped me to understand the lights and colours I could see everywhere. Until this point I had never really understood the importance of each colour, its shade or density. Valerie quizzed me over my own personal experiences and I told her of the lights that I could see around everything. She listened to me intently for half an hour or so and then explained to me that these lights were called auras and that they were an energetic representation of a person's emotional and physical state of being. I told her that they had been nothing other than a complete distraction for me, and asked if she could show me how I could best apply this new piece of knowledge. How could it help me better understand the healing process?

Valerie asked a friend of hers called Simon to come over to the healing group and asked him to stand up against a white wall. I was told to describe in detail the colours or shapes that I could see, feel or be aware of around him. I must explain that by this age I'd finally developed a technique where, to a certain extent, I could block out the visual distraction of auras.

As a child, this control had been impossible for me, but as I had got older I had had to find some way to shut out this information, as it was the only way I could cope. However, in the current situation, I had to go through the process of switching this ability back on.

I sat calmly in a comfortable chair opposite Simon and started to relax more, to be able to clearly focus on his aura. For me, looking at someone's aura and describing it is both a visual and emotional experience. Not only do I see colours and lights but I actually feel them too, like subtle shifts of energy. It's a bit like watching a play: you have the visual experience of the actors and their performance, but reach a point (if it's a good play), where you actually get emotionally involved. You start to feel what the actors are experiencing as if you're becoming them.

I will attempt to describe how I switch on this ability to see an aura. As I relax in a chair I shift my focus and awareness to the soles of my feet. My feet start to feel heavier and 'grounded' and as I focus my concentration, the energy beneath my feet starts to travel up my legs, into my hips, along my spine and right up to the crown of my head.

My crown starts to tingle, as if someone has gently placed their hands on the top of my head. Sometimes I can feel a slight pressure on my head when this happens. Then I focus on the energy in the palms of my hands and allow the energy to travel up my arms, into my shoulders and connect up with the same point at the crown.

It feels like I am literally sucking in energy through the soles of my feet and palms of my hands and this energy is being sent to the crown area. I then let my eyes blur and go slightly out of focus and when I do this, the colours and shapes of the aura start to appear. The more I relax into this feeling, the clearer the colours and lights become. It is at this point that I am able to describe what I can see and feel.

When I studied Simon's aura I could see a glowing, misty, blue light emanating from his head and shoulders. This light reduced in intensity and fluorescence as it tapered down his body. On his left shoulder I could see a darker area that was round, dull and a bit greenish and grey in colour.

I mentioned this to Valerie and she asked me what I thought it meant. I thought about this for a moment and studied this area some more. It reminded me of a cloud, or a shadow of a cloud on an otherwise clear, sunny day. I knew it was a marker of some kind and Valerie said that it was an indication of a problem area.

I was a bit sceptical of this statement and so I asked Simon if he had a problem with his left shoulder. When he said that he did, I grew really excited because this meant that I might be able to detect physical ailments by examining a person's aura. I was very eager and inspired at this point and I wanted to investigate it a lot further, so I examined the auras of everyone present in the room.

I accurately managed to detect and diagnose all the physical ailments that they were aware of, including some that they were not. Nowadays, because of my experience in reading and understanding auras, I am also able to analyse emotional states of being and, in some cases, I can go as far as knowing what has happened to a person in the past.

Valerie then described to me the whole healing process that Cain and the others used. Normally they would ask a patient to lie down on the floor in a comfortable position, on cushions or a soft rug for example. The healer would either place their hands on the crown or six inches from the crown of the patient's head, relax and allow energy to flow through their body. The healer would then slowly move their hands around the patient's body, moving down the shoulders, arms, torso, legs and feet.

This entire process could take anything from ten to twenty minutes. I asked Valerie why it was necessary for the healer to make physical contact with the patient and she told me that it was her belief that it probably wasn't that imperative. In most cases it only reinforced the bond between the healer and patient, strengthening the physical connection as well as making the patient feel safer and more secure. More recently, as I have become used to giving healing to large crowds of people, I have found that it is quite unnecessary for me to physically touch a patient and would only do so under certain circumstances.

I have grown to believe physical touching in this way is only necessary to remove a stubborn energy blockage or for reassurance purposes, and that if a patient feels secure with their healer and environment then there is usually no need for it.

Valerie knew that I had an unusual ability: by concentrating on a person's arms or legs they would spontaneously move. I wanted to know if she thought this ability could be put to good use in the healing process.

First of all, Valerie asked me to describe my thoughts and feelings at such times. What did I believe I was doing when I caused a person's arms or legs to move? What was it that I actually did and how did I do it? I had to think very hard about this.

I have a process which involves tapping into energy, in a similar way to how I see auras. I can project this energy into the body of the person, but this only works if they give me their permission to do so. As I transmit this energy, basically I tell the energy exactly what I want it to do by giving it a very simple command, like "lift up your arm to shoulder level now". Usually within a couple of seconds the person's arm moves. If it was only moving really slowly then I'd push out more energy towards them and tell it to work faster, and in return it usually would.

Valerie said that in her opinion I was very lucky as I had unknowingly managed to master, control and regulate the level of energy I was transmitting. When I projected this energy towards another, telling it to raise a person's arm or leg, she wondered what would happen if I told the energy to correct a physical problem or remove the pain instead. For me, this was a remarkable suggestion. Could it possibly be that simple? The only way I could find out would be to try it and so I asked Simon if he minded being a guinea-pig. Simon had practised healing himself, he was intrigued with what was going on and was happy for me to try.

I asked Valerie to stand behind Simon who was facing me approximately four feet away. I concentrated on Simon and transmitted energy towards him, then in my mind I told this energy to give Simon what he needed and to correct the physical problem in his left shoulder as fast as possible. We waited for about twenty seconds before anything happened, then Simon's left arm started to rise up on its own.

At this point I didn't believe that anything in particular was happening to his shoulder. This was nothing new for me: I'd seen this kind of spontaneous movement a thousand times before. But past the point of comfort, Simon's arm kept on moving, past elbow height and as far as shoulder height. Now this action started to look quite different: his fingers stretched upwards and outwards as he reached right over his head and towards his right. As it happened, Simon said that he felt warm sensations moving through his left arm and into his shoulder. When I heard this I transmitted an increased amount of energy and Simon noticed I had done this because he said that his shoulder had suddenly become much hotter. It seemed that from then on the more energy I sent, the hotter Simon's arm and shoulder became.

Simon said that the heat felt deep and intense, thoroughly warming and not a bit uncomfortable. It then reached the point when he told me that it was so hot his shoulder pain seemed to just melt away. As soon as he said this his arm stretched upwards as far as it would go, then backwards and down in a circle. This movement repeated itself a further three times until his arm finally came to rest of its own accord. At the end of this whole exercise Simon took great delight in telling us all that he was now completely without pain.

After this initial experience, Simon was intrigued by the fluidity and flexibility of his arm and shoulder, because previously he hadn't been able to exercise it at all. Apparently he had had difficulty raising it beyond shoulder height and reaching for the sky had been nearly impossible. This new pain-free movement was wonderful for him. I was very pleased and excited by my first real healing experience and decided to join the group and attend regular weekly sessions. I now knew that I had to endeavour to expand and investigate the possibilities that lay behind my own healing potential.


Outside the healing group, my other friends had difficulty understanding and accepting what they considered to be my strange and spooky activities. I'd explained it to them many times, but it was totally beyond them why I would want to spend three nights a week with a bunch of strange hippie-students and they mercilessly ribbed and teased me about it.

My dad's work had grown quite considerably over the years and he had built up a reputable wholesale business selling handbags and leather goods. Hence it seemed natural for both my brother and I to go and work for him after school was over.

Three months went by before the other members of my family found out about these healing sessions and then they joined in too. They made fun of me to the point where they challenged my sanity, and it was obvious that the fact that I had a 'normal' or 'proper' job was my only saving grace.

Over the next four months I was subjected to a barrage of comments and jokes before I eventually succumbed under the pressure and decided it would be best if I stopped healing. Everybody told me that it was the common sense and right thing to do. Knuckling down and getting on with earning some money and building my career would be best for me in the long run. Ironically, though, from this moment on, the particular friends and family members who persuaded me to give up my healing at this point in my life were the very ones who would rush back to me at a moment's notice with every little ache and pain.

Ten years went by. Although I appreciated the perks of having a good job and money in my pocket, I also felt restricted. I knew that there was something seriously missing in my life. I grew more and more bored and disheartened at the prospect of spending the rest of my life selling handbags and I finally decided to go on a journey of self-discovery. Israel, the place of my birth, seemed like a good place to start.

I didn't know what I was looking for, nor did I have any expectations. At this time, I was purely drifting without direction and the only thing I knew was that I had to get away from this daily rut I was in. I stayed with my Uncle Dov and Aunt Miriam in a small village, forty minutes drive from Tel Aviv. Time was on my hands and I needed something to do, so I decided to attempt to re-learn Hebrew. But mostly I wandered, contemplating the rest of my life and what on earth I would do on my return to England.

I had been in Israel for around six months and it was nearly time for me to return. As my departure grew closer, I became more and more anxious. I still hadn't found any answers for myself. One evening, as I lay on my bed, I felt quite desperate and so I asked for help. I didn't know who I was asking, whether it was God or another part of myself, but my question was clear: What should I do? What was my purpose? I wanted to become aware of my best purpose, and now I truly believe that this was the first time in my life that I had accidentally made a connection with my Higher Self. I meditated and contemplated this question for several hours until I finally drifted off to sleep.

The following morning at breakfast, my Uncle came into the kitchen carrying a crate of oranges. He was moaning and complaining about his back and neck. As I helped him with the crate, he told me that the pain came in waves, that he'd been x-rayed some time ago and that the doctors had diagnosed him with worn vertebrae in the neck. The discomfort was something he suffered in silence. As far as he was concerned, nothing could be done about it as his condition was due to general wear and tear.

I told my Uncle that I used to heal some years ago. It never crossed my mind that I could fix his problem, but I did think that I might be able to do something to help his pain. Dov said that on a bad day like this he was willing to try anything so I sat him down in a chair in the kitchen.

In this instance, I put my right hand on the back of his neck and my left hand on his shoulder and chest area at the front of his body. I relaxed and concentrated and tried to send him some healing energy, my primary concern being to remove the symptoms of his pain and give him some relief. Dov said that he couldn't feel any heat or anything at all, which I thought was a bit strange, but I continued working with him like this for about twenty minutes.

After I had finished, I asked Dov how he felt. Had the pain gone or was it at least a bit better? Dov was disappointed for both of us. His pain was as bad as ever. He confessed that he had really wanted it to work, but that he wasn't going to lie to me and tell me that it had when it hadn't. I was quite depressed about this, and reasoned that as I had ignored my healing for so long then I had lost the ability, or worse, perhaps it had been taken away from me.

All that day I grew more and more anxious, to the point where I felt panicky. Dov went about his usual business, determined to grin and bear it, and I experienced a combination of emotions heavily laden with guilt. One thing was for sure; my choices were now fewer. I had asked for guidance on my true purpose and the very next day found out that my abilities had vanished. Was this God's way of telling me to just get on with my life?

The following morning I woke up as usual with the sun pouring into my room when Uncle Dov burst in. He was excited, elated in fact. For the first time in years he'd woken up feeling wonderful: his pain had gone, not just a bit, but completely. Amazingly, he'd experienced a 24-hour delay to my healing. Such delays have happened since, but only on the odd occasion.

When Aunt Miriam realised what had happened she quickly spread the news throughout the rest of the family and close community. Her nephew was a healer! She invited everyone who had any kind of physical ache or pain to the house, which quickly turned into nothing short of a surgery. I didn't mind doing this. I was still in a state of inner confusion, but I at least felt good about the fact that I was doing something worthwhile and positive. For the first time in a long time, I felt happy, I was pleased that I could be of help and it tickled me to see my Aunt and Uncle take so much pride in what I was endeavouring to do. It was also very good practice for me.

I would like now to attempt to describe the healing method I used at this time. Imagine a river of invisible energy that flows around the body and that to the touch this energy feels like touching a fine cushion of air. If there is a physical problem in the body, then it will create a kind of bump or hole in this energy field.

If I were to place my hand over one of these bumps, it would feel like my hand was being pushed away - a similar feeling to the repelling sensations created by the same two poles of a magnet. When my hands found a hole in the energy field, the energy would pull at my hand, like the two opposite poles of a magnet, and my hand would be drawn towards the body. Here it would be necessary to touch the body of the patient.

Usually, the place where I found a hole in the energy field would be the point of pain for the patient, and so when I found a hole I would concentrate on it and try to put more energy into it. Slowly, as the energy filled the hole, I would begin to feel my hand being pushed away from the body. Eventually as the problem was being corrected my hand would rise up in line with the rest of the body's energy field, the idea being that I would endeavour to get the patient's energy field smooth and even. I'd be, in effect, pushing the bumps down and filling up the holes. Afterwards, I would sweep with my hands to check the smoothness of the energy field.

The people I gave healing to while in Israel responded to it immediately. My Uncle Dov still remained the exception. Most of the ailments, however, were of a physical nature and joint- or muscle-related. Then one day, shortly before my return to England, I was asked to help my Uncle Ezra who had been seriously injured in one of the numerous wars that plague the Middle East.

He had been regularly attending a pain clinic at the local hospital and although this had helped to reduce his discomfort marginally, he was still suffering very badly and experiencing a high level of pain twenty-four hours a day. He had received a nasty stab injury to his middle back and due to the severity of his wound I was very unsure of my ability to help him. His problem was much more serious than those I had treated and the doctors had said that he would most likely suffer a high level of pain, possibly for the rest of his life.

My lack of confidence was due to my own scepticism about the healing process. I believed at that time that a lot of it was psychological. In other words, the patients believed that I could heal them and it was this belief that removed their problem. Even though the pain in my Uncle Dov's neck and back still hadn't returned, I continued to believe that whatever I did was only a temporary measure and that once the harsh reality of the patient's problem hit home, the symptoms of their pain would return. I could not accept at this time the possibility that in certain circumstances the body was capable of making a total recovery regardless of the extent of the injury or problem. Therefore I desperately needed encouragement from my Aunt and Uncle before I could even think about attempting to help Uncle Ezra.

They all urged me to try. I was very apprehensive when I placed my hands on the top of Ezra's head and followed my usual method of healing, levelling off the bumps and holes in the energy field around his body. When I reached the point of his injury I tried to really concentrate and boost into this area as much energy as possible. As I physically placed my hands on his back and kept them there for about five minutes, Ezra said that he could feel a little bit of heat coming through. Then slowly I pulled my hands away from his body and held them there approximately eight inches away and concentrated intensely.

Within a couple of minutes I realised that Ezra had fallen into a deep sleep. We had been chatting a little throughout this and I chuckled a bit to myself, assuming that he must have got bored with my conversation and nodded off. I continued for a few more minutes, then left to congregate with the others in the kitchen for a coffee and let Ezra rest for as long as he needed to.

A couple of hours later Ezra woke up and called me into his room. He claimed to be completely pain-free. I thought he was just being polite - this was how sceptical I was - and in a frank exchange I challenged him to be honest with me. He insisted he was telling the truth, that his pain had gone and we fell into a deep conversation.

He wanted to know exactly what I was going to do on my return to England. He knew that I was bored with my job and career and he urged me to look into the possibilities of healing others on more of a full-time basis. He was very adamant that his pain relief wasn't in his mind and that I genuinely did have something to offer. Throughout this discussion I was fairly distracted, constantly waiting for his pain to return. I just felt that it would come back any second and so I stayed around for several hours to see. The following day, I telephoned him to see how he was and much to his delight and my relief he said that he was still without pain.

The day I was leaving for England, which was about two weeks later, Ezra called me to say 'thank you'. He confirmed that his pain hadn't returned and he urged me again to look into the possibilities of pursuing a healing career. Although I had had a lot of success in healing others in Israel, my confidence in myself and my abilities on my return to England was still very low. I was reluctant to tell my family about what had happened. On the occasions when I tried, I was still met with total scepticism and disbelief and this attitude continued to shatter my confidence. Five months later, my father returned from a short holiday in Israel. He and my mother had been staying with Dov and Miriam and had met up with Ezra at a family wedding. They had been told the whole story. On my father's return, he was finally convinced that my healing abilities were not just a figment of my imagination and that they could possibly be put to good use. For the first time he could see what it was I had been trying to do. He told me that if I wanted to pursue my healing on more of a full-time basis, if it was what I really wanted and needed to do, then he would support and back me all the way, both personally and financially.

My father believed at this point that even if I was very successful in healing, I would still never have the same kind of income I had been used to. He realised that certain sacrifices would have to be made. Materially, things would have to go. I wouldn't be able to afford the nice car I had been used to, for instance, and from then on I would have to be careful with what money I had. However, he said that if I were serious about this, he would help me as and when he could and he gave me the back-up support that I really needed.

As I was making this huge commitment, I wanted as much guidance and advice as possible. Once again, I asked God, (or myself, I don't know) for help. The next day I was driving through Bury in Lancashire and as I drove up a particular street I noticed several signs advertising a whole range of clinics specialising in treatments such as physiotherapy, dental practice, acupuncture and osteopathy. One in particular drew my attention as it listed a whole range of treatments that were not familiar to me at the time, such as craniosacral therapy and reflexology. I decided to pull in and have a look. I parked my car and wandered about, reading the boards and practices of each clinic. I didn't know what I was looking for exactly, but I followed a gut feeling and decided to take the plunge and investigate one particular practice. This was all done on impulse - I hadn't dressed for any kind of interview and I was wearing jeans, trainers and a T-shirt. I had no idea what kind of response I was going to get, if any.

Nervously, I asked the receptionist if I could speak to the person in charge of the clinic. I had to wait a while, until I was greeted by a friendly woman whom I shall call Karen. Later she told me that she was qualified in a range of professions, such as reflexology, physiotherapy and osteopathy and she explained to me that she had entered into alternative healing after having several minor operations herself that hadn't been successful.

We went through the usual introductions and I took the

plunge and told her about myself and what I believed I could do. I didn't think that she would really take me all that seriously, but to my surprise she responded very positively to what I had to say, showing only mild signs of scepticism. She confessed that in her own experience, on the odd occasion in her normal or usual treatments, positive things had happened to her patients that she couldn't find any logical explanation for. So she was open to all forms of alternative healing and welcomed the possibilities.

Her very next session was with a patient who had been suffering the symptoms of a very debilitating disorder called motor neuron disease. He had been attending her clinic for several months and Karen had been trying to help him relieve some of his pain. Karen asked him if he would be interested in meeting me and, as he was in extreme discomfort, he said that he would do anything if she thought it would help him.

Karen invited me into the treatment room and introduced me to the patient, whom I shall call Martin. I explained to him what I did and that I was prepared to see if I could help him, although I didn't want to build up his expectations. Martin was already lying on the treatment couch. Karen naturally remained in the room at all times, comforting and assisting him.

I began the process in my usual way by levelling off the bumps and filling up the holes in his energy field, which felt very weak to me. It took about twenty minutes to complete and then I asked him how he was feeling. Martin said that he felt as if his pain had decreased by about sixty-five percent. He was really happy about this but I was a bit disappointed that I hadn't been able to remove it altogether. However Karen told me that due to the serious nature of his condition and his constant high level of pain, this was an excellent result and that I should be very pleased.

Karen genuinely wanted to help those who were sick or in pain and she was impressed with Martin's new and improved condition. She asked me if I would be prepared to test out my abilities on some of her other patients and I was delighted at the prospect of being able to do this. It was my first opportunity to work in a fully equipped therapy centre under professional supervision and receive expert guidance.

Over the next three months I treated a multitude of conditions, from frozen shoulders and bad backs to knee and joint problems. Some of these conditions were quite severe. Throughout this time I refined my healing techniques and the ability to detect the precise origin of a problem. Often Karen would bring me into her surgery to consult me in the diagnostic process. With practice I was now able to pinpoint accurately where the cause of the problem was, by either feeling the patient's energy field or scanning their aura. I had no idea at this time what the problems were; I could just detect where they were. But the information I was able to provide speeded up Karen's ability to help her patients.

It was a well-equipped, nicely decorated clinic, with a wall clock in every treatment room and corridor. My concentration levels throughout this period were naturally very high and unavoidably I managed to break all the clocks in the building. I regularly fused the lights and unknowingly sent power surges through the equipment. In the kitchen appliances blew, the cooker wouldn't work and the kettle and toaster broke. It became a bit embarrassing and Karen would constantly tease me, saying that I might be good at healing but that I was costing her a fortune! I don't know if I was responsible for all these mishaps, but I certainly carried the blame.

The reactions to my healing were all very positive, but still I wasn't convinced. Being a very logical person I concluded that I simply could be having a 'placebo' effect on the patients. The turning point was when Karen introduced me to a patient of hers whom I shall call Sarah.

I had talked about my feelings, lack of confidence and scepticism with Karen at great length. She was actually much more convinced of my abilities than I was. Because I doubted myself so much, Karen knew that I could be put off easily and she decided not to tell me about the seriousness and nature of Sarah's problem. All Karen told me was that Sarah had been in a lot of pain with a back complaint and that I should simply do my best!

As Sarah lay on the treatment couch chatting quietly to Karen, I went through my usual healing process starting from the crown of her head. I followed the energy field around her body, removing the bumps and holes as I went. Seconds after I had started, Sarah said that she could feel a comforting but intense heat throughout her entire body, especially in her lower back and spine.

When I came to her right hip area I felt a huge hole in her energy field and knew instantly that the main cause of her problem was here. I concentrated intensely on this part of her energy field, pumping as much of my energy into this hole as I could. Suddenly her body started to twitch and jerk slightly. Her muscles were in spasm, particularly around the lower back and hip area, and it was obvious to me that this was creating even more pain for her. When I saw all this movement, combined with the fact that she was in a lot of discomfort, I turned to Karen for support. I must have looked worried, because she instantly responded telling me that she had expected something like this to happen and that I must continue. Sarah also reassured me - she could handle the pain if it meant getting a positive result. So I carried on. Thirty seconds later, Sarah's entire body relaxed and went limp. Calmly she told me that all the pain had now gone and that she felt fine. It took me another five minutes or so to finish the healing process, smoothing out the energy field around the rest of her body.

After I had finished I asked her if it was possible for her to get up off the couch; to stand up and tell me how she felt. Tentatively she sat up and swung both legs off the couch; as she placed her right foot on the floor there was a thud. Sarah stood up. She seemed stunned and excited. Karen also looked thrilled and amazed. As Sarah put all her weight onto both feet and stood up, expectation hung silently in the air.

Sarah started to giggle uncontrollably, and then as she looked at Karen she started to cry. At this point Karen was practically in tears herself and seemed mesmerised. I wondered what on earth was going on. I asked them what the big deal was and it was at this point that Karen told me that since the age of three Sarah hadn't been able to place both feet flat on the floor at the same time. For fourteen years Sarah had undergone many operations on her right hip because she had contracted TB as a child. The doctors also found that one of her legs had been growing longer than the other.

As a child they had tried to correct this with surgery but the operation had had a reverse effect and Sarah's right leg was now shorter than her left one. Sarah also had a curvature of the spine.

When Karen explained all this to me I became more confused. Did she honestly expect me to believe that Sarah's leg had suddenly grown? In her attempt to illustrate what had happened, Karen asked Sarah if she would mind lying back down on the couch again. As Sarah did this she told me that all her pain had gone and that she really couldn't believe what was happening.

Karen asked if I had noticed the positioning of Sarah's knees before I had started the healing process and I had to confess that I hadn't. Now, as I looked, I could see that one knee was approximately two inches higher than the other, which to me proved that her legs hadn't grown at all. Karen explained that Sarah had a curvature in her spine, which bent her body in such a way that exaggerated the difference in the length of her legs. During the healing process her spine had straightened, allowing her hips to level and the result was that she could now put both feet firmly on the ground.

Karen then asked Sarah if she could get up and walk around the room. As she did this, I noticed that she had a slight limp and commented on it. Sarah responded, laughing, she said that before she had literally had to hop to get about. This slight limp was a tremendous improvement for her and it was such a relief to be finally rid of her pain.

As Sarah happily demonstrated her new walking abilities to both of us, her mother entered the room. The sun was shining through the blinds (it was a lovely summer's day) and Sarah's mom was still wearing her sunglasses. Sarah was just about bursting she was so overjoyed. Naturally she showed off her walking to her mother and hurriedly told her what had happened. I happily watched all of this from the back of the room, noticing mom's tears behind the dark glasses. It was a really wonderful moment and one that I shall remember for the rest of my life.

It was at this point that I fell into the ego trap. Unfortunately, after this experience I became rather full of myself, believing that if I could straighten a curved spine, then I could heal anyone of anything, and this misguided belief was disastrous for me. I look back now and cringe! I must have been totally intolerable and, even though I can laugh about it now, I'm still appalled with my behaviour. I am ashamed to say that for four days I acted like the new messiah, then on the fifth day it hit me like a ton of bricks. My ego plummeted, as suddenly, for no reason, I was unable to correct even the simplest of problems. No matter what I did or how hard I tried my efforts were wasted. I had lost the ability to heal.

My self-confidence and self-esteem took a serious nose-dive but with this shift in perspective my ability to heal gradually resurfaced. I now know that this was my Higher Self's way of protecting me from my own ego. Up until this point in my life, I had believed that I was responsible for the healing and, understandably I suppose at the time, I thought I was great. This new found perspective, however, taught me that healing comes from a place far beyond the conscious mind, beyond normal perception. It comes from the Higher Self.

Over the next few months, as I treated patients for a variety of ailments, they started to respond to the healing I gave them with strange physical movement. Sometimes this could become quite bizarre: everything from twitching and jerking to limbs spontaneously rising in the air. Some started to tap themselves or wave their arms about, making big swirling gestures. It got to the point where nothing really surprised me. I was interested in documenting as much as I could and so with their permission I started to videotape various patients as they went through their corrections.

I was invited to talk about my psychic abilities by the Institute of Hypnosis and Parapsychology at a venue in Derby. I was terribly nervous about doing this as it was the first time I had spoken in public. After tentatively making my introduction, I asked the seventy or so people in the audience if they would like to watch a ten-minute film, which was a compilation of clips from various healing sessions.

Sure enough, as I approached the video system I was using, it spontaneously clicked on and surged into life. Because I was so nervous I was worried that I might inadvertently affect the TV and video equipment and when this suddenly happened my heart sank. Fortunately the film played all the way through without a glitch and then I started to relax into it.

The film was very well received and various members of the audience fired questions at me in their attempt to find an explanation for the healing that I practised and the spontaneous movements in my patients. At this point I decided to demonstrate on the audience as a whole to show them how it worked. This was totally unexpected, as most of the people present were only there to listen to what I had to say. I am a firm believer that action speaks louder than words: for me just talking about it is never enough. This was an ideal opportunity for believers and sceptics alike to personally experience this phenomenon on a physical level.

I invited a member of the audience to come up onto the stage. The gentleman in question was a rather tall hypnotherapist. As he made his way up I asked everyone to clear a space at the front of the stage and move the chairs away. I then asked for volunteers, anyone who thought or knew that they had a physical problem in their body. It didn't matter what it was, a creaky neck, frozen shoulder or bad back. I asked them to come to the front of the stage and stand in a line, like soldiers on parade.

Each volunteer had to bring a helper with them who was instructed to stand behind them for safety reasons. This was the first time I had demonstrated this on a large scale. I had to transmit a powerful energy signal and was conscious that there might be a few people present who would be especially sensitive to it. I needed to ensure that there was someone standing behind each volunteer just in case whatever it was I did made them feel dizzy or queasy.

This was very ambitious and something I decided to do on the spur of the moment. I was taking a huge chance: it was my first demonstration, I had never tried this on any more than two or three people at one time, and the audience consisted of specialists and parapsychologists. They had heard it all and seen it all before and I ran the risk of making a complete idiot of myself. However, I was strangely confident as somehow it just felt like the right thing to do.

The hypnotherapist who was on stage with me had a problem in his neck and sciatica in his lower back and I successfully detected this for him. It was my plan to try to correct this using a hands-on method and at the same time project my healing towards the volunteers who were standing in a row approximately twelve feet away from me.

I look back on this episode now and wonder why on earth I wanted to make things so difficult for myself. Treating one person at a time was hard enough with my level of experience then. Taking on up to thirty people at any one time was bordering on silly. We were all having a lot of fun though and everyone was having a good time and so I guess I just got a bit carried away.

I began what I can only describe as an energy projection. In simple terms, when I do this I feel as if I am transmitting a signal in a similar way to a satellite or a beacon. Firstly I have to stimulate my own internal energy. This feels similar to when you get frightened or excited: it feels like an adrenaline rush. I have to build this up to a level where my hands, feet and then entire body start to tingle. I 'buzz': it's like having an electric current running through me. Then, using my mind, I project this energy outwards and push it onto the person standing in front of me and within a few seconds their body spontaneously moves as it tries to correct any physical problems it had. You can often tell what is wrong with a person by the way their body involuntarily moves. For example, if the hips start to twist or turn, then it usually suggests that particular person has a lower back problem.

I projected my energy towards the audience concentrating on one volunteer at a time. It was a tremendous strain and it took a lot of effort and concentration, but as each person started to spontaneously move I would turn my attention to the next. Within ten minutes or so, the volunteers were all either moving or feeling shifts of energy throughout their body.

Only a couple of people said to me afterwards that they didn't feel as if they had responded, but interestingly enough many of the helpers who were standing behind the volunteers went into spontaneous movement too. The whole event was really enjoyable and many people came to me to tell me that their physical problem had either corrected itself or that they were feeling noticeably better. This demonstration was the catalyst for me: I decided that I was now ready to open my own small clinic from home.

Within a short space of time, my local newspaper picked up on what I was doing and ran my story. It created a bit of interest in the surrounding community and north Manchester area and I became quite busy. During this time I found myself rather obsessed with questions. Just exactly what was I doing, why did it work and where did it come from? I wasn't willing to put it down to the 'paranormal', the inexplicable was unacceptable to me and I wanted answers.

I started to film more, and I tried several experiments. For example, I wanted to know if someone would respond to my energy signal if they were in another room or behind a wall and I found out that they did. I tested the distance; did it matter how far away a person was? I asked a friend to walk right down to the end of my road, a distance of about 100 metres and to take someone with them to stand behind them and act as a helper. I projected my energy signal towards them in an attempt to push them over. I found that distance made no difference; with the same amount of effort I could push my friend backwards and into the arms of their helper.

I continued healing person-to-person and then discovered that I could send my healing energy down the telephone. A lady from Glasgow called me and asked me if I could help with her frozen shoulder. It was the first time we'd spoken and as she introduced herself she told me that a friend had recommended me. I tried to correct her shoulder there and then. As I projected my energy signal down the telephone she grew quite excited and told me that her body had started to move by itself. Within a matter of minutes her shoulder was better. Her local newspaper ran this story and this attracted even more attention.

All the experiments that we performed at this time were interesting and exciting and as I gathered more and more information I came to realise that there were a number of people around the world, including healers, mystics and martial arts masters, who could trigger spontaneous movement and healing in others. Then, in 1994, I made an astounding breakthrough which was to change my life forever. It was totally accidental, but it removed the veil of mystery surrounding the healing process. It led me to the development of a system in which each individual could empower themselves with the gifts and abilities of the gurus and mystics.

It changed my way of thinking and my whole perception, and opened the door to a whole new learning experience.

One day in April I asked a friend of mine called Costa to come and look at some new footage I had taken. The video film was mostly of myself projecting my energy signal in an attempt to initiate self-healing and featured the spontaneous movement and responses of those around me.

Costa, who is a member of the Institute of Hypnosis and

Parapsychology, was naturally intrigued and on several occasions previously he'd helped me conduct various simple experiments. He was standing around in my living room watching the film and I left to make a cup of tea. When I came back into the room I noticed that Costa was moving strangely. I laughed and I asked him what was going on, because I thought he was joking. He just shook his head and smiled incredulously and said that as he had been standing there watching the video, his body had just started to move on its own. He wanted to know what I was up to. Had I been projecting my signal from the kitchen? I told him that I'd been making the tea, that I wasn't responsible for it, and then it dawned on me that somehow the video must have triggered spontaneous self-healing in him.

Suddenly, the possibility that the video was responsible for this self-corrective process dawned on us. To take away any possible visual suggestion from the video, Costa turned around and stood with his back to the TV set. However his movements only became stronger.

We then tried other things - we turned the sound off, we dimmed and blacked-out the picture, but it made no difference and he still continued to respond. We decided at this point that we needed to test this on a larger scale and see what, if anything, would happen.

Costa had taken a stand at the Manchester Mind, Body, Spirit Festival and he said that this would be an ideal opportunity to try it out on some volunteers. On the first day, we ran the tape. I felt really stupid asking passers-by if they would be prepared to stand there and relax a bit, with their backs to a TV monitor. Naturally they wanted to know what it was all about and all I would tell them was that it was perfectly safe and nothing untoward would happen. Because I would offer no further explanation, it was quite difficult initially to get anyone to agree. Eventually I managed to get five people to try it at the same time.

Three out of the five people started to move spontaneously, four said that they felt nice warm sensations and the two that didn't move said that they could feel heat and internal fluttering (shifts of energy). The three volunteers that moved said that their hands felt tingly, as if they were mildly buzzing, and we discovered that they all had either back or neck problems. One of the volunteers that could feel the fluttering had a digestion problem.

The experiment attracted massive interest. There were several spectators who were intrigued with what was going on, but as this phenomenon was totally new to me I could tell them very little about it. Many of those watching didn't actually put two and two together, because the volunteers were standing with their backs to the TV monitor. Then, much to our amusement, some of the spectators said that they could feel themselves responding too and wanted to know how we were doing this! When I told them that the video was responsible, they didn't believe me. Soon it seemed as if everyone wanted to join in. By the middle of the afternoon, Costa couldn't get onto his stand as we were so busy, and neighbouring stand-holders were complaining about the log jam of people.

The next day the papers got hold of the story and before I knew it my face was on the front page of the Manchester Evening News. Over the next three days at the exhibition, approximately 550 people tried this experiment and experienced the physical effects of the video. Only eight people in total were unable to feel anything at all. The rest experienced various responses, from a general improvement in their well being, to dramatic positive physical changes. I had been invited to give a talk and simple demonstration in a separate part of the hall, and during this Costa still ran the experiment for me on his stand. The effects were the same; I didn't need to be present at all.

After the exhibition, I received many letters and calls of thanks from these people, claiming that after they had stood with their backs to the TV monitor their aches and pains, disorders and physical complaints had either been cured or dramatically improved. I couldn't get over this. I was both astounded and delighted and was very excited about pursuing the possibilities of using the video to initiate self-healing in others.

But at the same time I was puzzled. How could the video be causing these responses without the need for me to be present? I had to find out why. I racked my brains and tried to pick at the puzzle in a logical and scientific way. We had a video with sound and picture, but as our volunteers had all been standing with their backs to the picture, we knew that it couldn't be this. The only sound on the video was background noise - there were no words or suggestions. However it didn't appear to make any difference to the volunteers whether the sound was on or off. They still responded to the healing signal with spontaneous movement or felt unusual sensations in their bodies.

We pursued this further and copied this soundtrack onto audiocassette. A few friends and colleagues tried listening to this tape for me, both on a stereo system and personal Walkman. The effects were still the same. At one point, a friend of mine had his headphones on, waiting to see what would happen when he listened to the audio tape. Within moments, his arms started to spontaneously rise and he was amazed at how this could happen. However, in this instance I had accidentally forgotten to press the play button and so this foxed me even more!

We did everything possible to remove any suggestion from our unsuspecting friends and volunteers, but it didn't appear to make any difference how or where the audio and visual tape was played: we always got a response of some kind.

A friend of mine, Deborah, wanted to try the exercise. She was casually standing holding a copy of the audiocassette, waiting for Costa to put some new batteries into the Walkman. Deborah was in a relaxed frame of mind, but all of a sudden she said that she could feel tingling in her arms. Within seconds her body started to gently sway and her arms lifted up. At that moment, we realised that the responses had nothing to do with the sound or the picture. Somehow my healing signal had penetrated and was stored on the magnetic tape of the video and audiocassette!

I agreed to give a series of demonstrations at an exhibition in Cyprus and really wanted to try and make my healing signal available to those that needed it. Producing hundreds of videos or audiocassettes didn't seem to me to be very practical as not only could they be quite expensive to produce but they could also be easily copied. At that time, I didn't know whether this energy signal I transmitted could be misused at all and I didn't want to do anything irresponsible. So I decided to lock away the videos and cassettes and find another more suitable, easy to use and practical method for the individual which couldn't be copied.

Costa's friend Stephanie suggested that I attempt to store my energy signal onto a credit card, because that had a magnetic strip on the back. I thought she was joking, the very idea sounded ludicrous to me. I didn't believe that such a small strip of magnetic tape would be able to retain the energy signal. The video and audiocassettes that we had been using were at least an hour long so how could less than two inches of magnetic tape possibly achieve the same effect? And anyway, even if it could, I didn't believe that it would work. It sounded preposterous.

Costa very subtly reminded me that it was all quite laughable and with a smirk said that it was at least worth a try. I couldn't dispute this, so for the next fifteen minutes I projected my signal and in effect attempted to 'heal' Costa's Barclaycard! The sarcasm and teasing was rife between us as I went through this process. I then handed it to him to try. As Costa held the card in his right hand, within moments both his arms spontaneously rose up to shoulder level. Even I had to admit that the card appeared to work better than the video cassette.

Over the next few weeks I made about a thousand new cards with a magnetic strip on the back and for want of a better name I simply called them 'Cobycards'. I took the cards to Cyprus with me, as an aid to help me with my demonstrations, but I also wanted an opportunity to test out the cards on a large scale.

At most of my demonstrations I get a mixed group of people who come along to see what I do. I would say that fifty percent usually have some kind of physical or emotional problem, the rest are made up of the curious and interested, with only a small number of total sceptics and disbelievers. My demonstrations in Cyprus were no exception.

About sixty people at a time would attend each demonstration and I used a mixture of my own personal energy signal and the Cobycard. When I send out my personal energy signal I simultaneously transmit a telepathic message to the person or people in front of me, telling their body to activate the healing process. Through trial and error, I found out that the Cobycard worked much better and more consistently if the person holding it literally told their body to heal.

At the demonstration in Cyprus, on average approximately four people out of the total number present wouldn't respond to either the card or myself. At this time however, I didn't truly understand how to use the Cobycard properly and I couldn't figure out why it worked for most, but not for everyone. To this day I don't really know why most people respond, some rather dramatically, but yet still a few don't or can't for some reason. Wanting something or believing in it bears no relevance. Time and time again it is often the case that the few individuals who don't respond, fully believe in what I am doing and desperately want it to work for themselves.

At this time I formed a small organisation (Zvikler Healing Research) to look into and investigate this phenomenon. The Cobycard developed in design from a simple credit card to a circular disc that could be worn around the neck. It still had the magnetic strip on the back and was three times stronger than the card. I called this the 'Power Disc' and over a period of about ten months distributed about a thousand of them to people who approached me with both physical and emotional problems.

The Power Disc was capable of triggering spontaneous self-healing in a person but there were still some problems with the magnetic strip. I was unable to increase the power or effectiveness of the Power Disc. While it was effective for a lot of people, I felt that some people needed a stronger signal. We also found that if the wearer came too close to another magnetic or electrical field the signal could scramble and stop the Power Disc from working properly.

I received several calls from people complaining that the

codes and information on their personal credit cards had been wiped and their cards had been rendered useless. This lack of permanence and consistency concerned me and I realised very quickly that using magnetic tape had its limitations. So I experimented to see if I could find another storage medium for the healing signal.

I looked at the possibilities of using gold, copper, silver, steel and chrome and found that it was possible to store the signal on gold and silver. However the cost of manufacturing gold or silver discs would have been really high and it seemed to defeat the point for me. I wanted a storage medium that would be economical to produce; thereby making it available to anybody who needed it, irrespective of their financial status.

A friend, who had been using the Power Disc, introduced me to the work of Nicoli Tesla, the inventor of many things including the AC alternating current. Apparently he had investigated the properties of aluminium as a storage medium for energy codes and frequencies. If I could use aluminium as the storage for my energy signal, it would solve many problems. I would be able to produce Discs very economically. If it worked, more than likely the energy codes would be retained within the aluminium on a permanent basis and not be susceptible to other influences such as a strong magnetic or electrical field.

I tried some very simple experiments using the aluminium ring-pulls from fizzy drink cans. Initially all the experiments seemed to fail because I used the same method and time frame for the Cobycards and Power Discs. I persevered though. It took ten days of focusing all my concentration and energy onto the aluminium ring-pulls before they retained any kind of signal at all. But after this period of time I realised the potential of the material and knew aluminium would be the best practical storage medium.

I designed a new disc made from aluminium and called it the 'Em-Power Disc'. Again, after trial and error, I found that I could charge these Discs in batches to a higher level and intensity to that of the Power Disc, but that it would take me a minimum of six weeks to do it. The Em-Power Discs are now seven times more powerful than the original Cobycard and I am able to gauge the strength of the signal by the speed and the intensity of a person's reaction.

Zvikler Healing Research has been looking into the effects of the Em-Power Disc for the past three years now. Several thousand people, with a variety of physical and emotional conditions are involved in compiling information. The most common problems have been joint- and muscle-related, skeletal and structural problems, pain relief, phobias, fear and anxiety; negative thought patterns and depression. We have had people with serious asthma, allergies, high blood pressure and ME.

All conditions have varied in degree and intensity: we are working with those who are sick and those who are very sick. When I started Em-Power Therapy, most people came to me as a last resort; they had tried conventional medicine and other forms of alternative healing but with little success. In my experience, if they are very ill some people can become quite desperate and no matter how bizarre the concept may appear, or how ridiculous it may sound, are prepared to try anything with a remote possibility of gaining a result.

However, as the Em-Power Healing System helped them, the word spread very rapidly to those around them who were not desperately ill but in need of treatment of some kind. The attitude towards what I was endeavouring to do changed quite dramatically. The seriously ill or injured who had gained benefit naturally recommended me to others and the interest grew rapidly, without the need to advertise or seriously promote myself.

There is also ongoing investigation by paranormal experts into the Em-Power Disc and my abilities. I have had several TV and radio interviews and given numerous public demonstrations. The Em-Power Disc works consistently and the nature of it enables the sceptical and disbelieving to participate personally rather than just commenting on what they see. I have demonstrated on presenters, reporters and whole film crews at the same time, to enable them to get a more personal view over what's happening in their body. In nearly every case they do not expect to physically respond to the Disc and when they do they become even more interested, but also mystified, as if they are in awe of their reactions.

In the early days of the Cobycard I had no idea how I did what I did. I couldn't control the healing signal I was transmitting, or regulate it. Over the last few years, as I have learned to control my abilities more and as I have collated information regarding the self-healing process, many fascinating and remarkable insights have been revealed.

While previously I would have had to describe the process as mystical and paranormal, I now feel that there is a logical explanation for most of the phenomena that exists in the paranormal world. However, I still cannot explain in words the mental and physical process that I use when I create the Em-Power Disc as it happens on an instinctive level. But I can tell you how and why it works, how we can benefit from using the Em-Power Disc, how we are able to initiate the self healing process, and what happens in our body and mind when we do so. These mysteries I can reveal.

All the information in this book is based on my own personal observations and experiences. Its contents can be put to the test by correct use of the Em-Power Disc. This demonstrates that we are all much more than just a physical body, that we are all able to tap into the hidden abilities that we possess. These are the very same abilities that have been described as 'paranormal' and beyond the reach of the average person.

The Em-Power Healing System has more recently evolved into a new and unique therapy. Not only does this system work on its own, on an individual level, but it is also a way of improving and enhancing other therapies. Em-Power Therapy is now being used in conjunction with conventional medicine as well as alternative medicine such as acupuncture, hypnotherapy, spiritual healing and reflexology.

Self-healing on a physical and emotional level is the primary function of the Em-Power Disc. People from all walks of life have been using the Disc to enhance and improve the quality of their lives, both at home and at work, including leisure and play. Many have claimed that by incorporating Em-Power Therapy into their lives they feel energised, and full of vitality.

I have found that we are all gifted and possess unlimited potential for self-development on all levels: physical, emotional, mental and spiritual. You might have a physical problem, such as a bad back or a repetitive strain injury, or want to stop smoking or lose some weight; you might have a phobia, suffer fear or anxiety, need some help learning a language or want to enhance your memory skills. Whatever your circumstances, the process of using Em-Power Therapy is quite simple once the principles are understood.

Em-Power Therapy can help expand awareness, bringing within reach the things you may have only dreamed about before. Many people now believe that the Em-Power Disc is a universal key to the inner world of the mind and body, unlocking the natural power that rests within all of us. By knowing and realising our own potential we are in a better position to take control of and make the most of our lives.

# PART II

INTERACTIVE COMMUNICATION USING
THE EM-POWER DISC

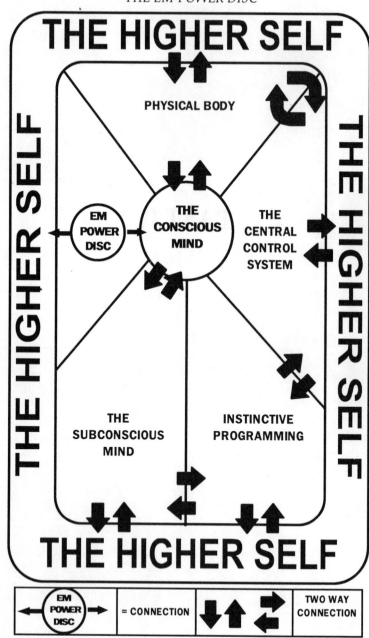

# INTRODUCING
# THE INTERACTIVE MIND MODEL

I have made some exciting discoveries over the past five years which have forced me to try to find better ways to explain how the Em-Power Disc works and to develop Em-Power Therapy to enhance the quality of life.

Em-Power Therapy is designed to allow the individual to communicate and interact with their body and mind in order to make positive changes on an emotional, physical and spiritual level. By expanding present day understanding of the mind and how it works, this book will help you realise your potential.

Through questioning the nature of our existence and our ability to adapt to our environment, the human race has been able to evolve substantially in a relatively short period of time. But, however amazing our accomplishments are in the field of science, technology and medicine, very little is known about the complexities of human consciousness. Medicine has dissected the brain; new and incredible diagnostic and scanning devices have mapped every aspect of the physical body in intricate detail. Yet the true essence of who and what we are always seems to elude us.

Em-Power Therapy allows us to discover, communicate and interact with not just the physical aspect of who we are, but with the very essence of our consciousness. It provides you with a unique simple and easy method of communication with a special part of your being, the Higher Self.

There is nothing new about the concept of the Higher Self. However, up until now it has been very difficult to prove its existence. The millions of years of human evolution and ancient wisdom that exists within the Higher Self has so far been an untapped resource. You now have the opportunity to unlock your true potential by communicating with your Higher Self, using Em-Power Therapy and the Em-Power Disc.

It is far easier to understand a whole subject or resolve a problem if you look at it in small sections. 'The Interactive Mind Model' is a very simple representation of human consciousness, which enables you to look at the various parts of the body and mind in an easy-to-digest way.

The model represents how our mind and body assimilate, store and process information on a moment-by-moment basis. It is very important to understand however, that every part of the body and mind is unique in its own way and it is how the individual aspects work as a whole that makes up a 'conscious being'.

As Em-Power Therapy is new for many readers, I do not feel it is appropriate to go into too much detail at this stage. As an intro-duction, I would rather concentrate on everyday situations and look at what happens within the mind and body on a moment-by-moment basis.

We shall determine how our emotions affect us and how our mind tries to process and analyse the information we receive through the five senses. By examining how negative thought patterns affect us, we can make the delicate shift needed to break free from old negative, emotional and physical baggage.

Awareness is the tool we need to let go of past negative thought processes, behaviours and cycles. I hope to illustrate how Em-Power Therapy can help you make the necessary changes and give you the ability to resolve these issues for yourself.

In the next section we shall investigate the various parts that make up the 'Interactive Mind Model', look at the flow of sensory information we receive and how it is processed.

# THE PARTS OF
# THE INTERACTIVE MIND MODEL
*(See diagram "Interactive Communication" page 36)*

**THE PHYSICAL BODY** is the 'housing' or instrument that allows us to experience our world through the five senses: sight, hearing, touch, taste and smell. This sensory information is passed to the conscious mind.

**THE CONSCIOUS MIND** tries to evaluate all the information it receives through the senses. After making its assessment, it deposits the information into the subconscious. The subconscious mind saves or records it in a similar way to the storage process of the hard drive of a computer.

**INSTINCTIVE PROGRAMMING and THE CENTRAL CONTROL SYSTEM.** Many aspects of the physical body run on a totally spontaneous level without any conscious effort. Information about these processes is contained within our **INSTINCTIVE PRO-GRAMMING.** This Instinctive Programming may be compared to DNA, 'the building blocks of life'. One part of our DNA is responsible for deciding on the way we look and determines our individual characteristics for example. Another part contains pre-recorded information that allows our bodies to function, self-regulate and 'grow' on a totally spontaneous and non-conscious level. We call this part the **CENTRAL CONTROL SYSTEM.**

**THE HIGHER SELF** *(sometimes called the Superconscious)* is a benevolent intelligence that we all possess. It is a highly advanced intellect, which has access to the blueprint of every aspect of our being. The Higher Self exists to serve as our guide and conscience through life and, some believe, beyond.

In summary, the various components of the Interactive Mind Model are THE PHYSICAL BODY, THE CONSCIOUS AND SUB-CONSCIOUS MIND, INSTINCTIVE PROGRAMMING, THE CENTRAL CONTROL SYSTEM and THE HIGHER SELF. It is very important to remember that the parts are interconnected and work together as a whole.

**The EM-POWER DISC** acts as a link between our conscious mind and the Higher Self and it allows us to communicate directly with the Higher Self in a new and unique way.

*THE CONSCIOUS MIND*

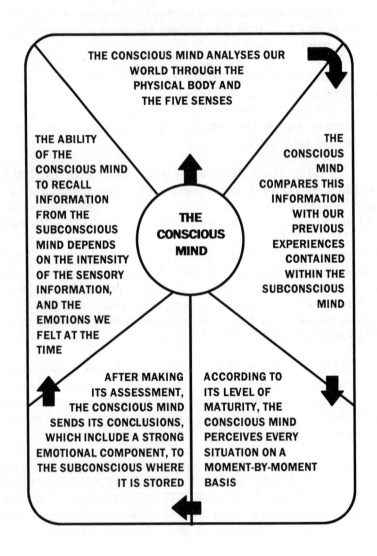

THE CONSCIOUS MIND ANALYSES OUR WORLD THROUGH THE PHYSICAL BODY AND THE FIVE SENSES

THE ABILITY OF THE CONSCIOUS MIND TO RECALL INFORMATION FROM THE SUBCONSCIOUS MIND DEPENDS ON THE INTENSITY OF THE SENSORY INFORMATION, AND THE EMOTIONS WE FELT AT THE TIME

THE CONSCIOUS MIND

THE CONSCIOUS MIND COMPARES THIS INFORMATION WITH OUR PREVIOUS EXPERIENCES CONTAINED WITHIN THE SUBCONSCIOUS MIND

AFTER MAKING ITS ASSESSMENT, THE CONSCIOUS MIND SENDS ITS CONCLUSIONS, WHICH INCLUDE A STRONG EMOTIONAL COMPONENT, TO THE SUBCONSCIOUS WHERE IT IS STORED

ACCORDING TO ITS LEVEL OF MATURITY, THE CONSCIOUS MIND PERCEIVES EVERY SITUATION ON A MOMENT-BY-MOMENT BASIS

*"HOW DOES THE CONSCIOUS MIND WORK?"*

# THE CONSCIOUS
# AND SUBCONSCIOUS MIND

*(See Diagram "The Conscious Mind" page 40)*
*and "The Subconscious Mind page 42)*

**The Conscious Mind** is a mechanism that assesses all situations before they are stored in the subconscious. Our consciousness develops over our whole lifetime but especially in our early years which is why, as children, we don't always assess a situation accurately. The child's conscious mind may not have matured sufficiently because it does not have enough 'life' experiences to refer to.

**The Subconscious Mind** stores all the information gathered through our life experiences. Each bit of information has a physical, emotional and sensory component. To take an example, think about eating a juicy, red apple. When we use our imagination in this way, our conscious mind is stimulated and it tries to find information associated with the apple in the subconscious - which is the sum of all our experiences. Provided that we have eaten an apple in the past, we can easily recall its shape, its texture, the way it felt when we bit into it, its taste and smell.

The conscious and subconscious team up to allow us to recall our experiences, and for this process to work they are both totally dependent on each other. Many of our present day problems (especially emotional ones) may be the result of something that has happened to us in the past, most likely as children.

Because our conscious mind is not fully developed at birth, many of our current problems are due to its inability to accurately assess and store its experiences within the subconscious. When we are children we go through the process of discovering our emotions and they become extremely sensitive. Because of this high emotional state, we feel things more powerfully as children than as adults.

At a young age we are mostly running on instinct, due to our lack of experiences. For example, imagine yourself as a child again, visiting the local shops with your mother. You let go of her hand to look into the grocer's window and as you do so, she steps inside, unnoticed. You are completely unaware that your mom has only walked a few yards into the shop, but because she has gone, your initial response at that young age would most likely be panic as the emotional umbilical cord has been visually severed. If this event happened as an adult, you would automatically just look around and investigate your immediate surroundings. You would make the assumption that if you couldn't see your mom and she was there moments ago, then

## THE SUBCONSCIOUS MIND

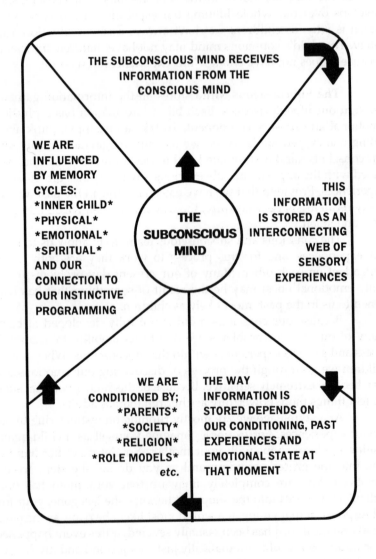

THE SUBCONSCIOUS MIND RECEIVES INFORMATION FROM THE CONSCIOUS MIND

WE ARE INFLUENCED BY MEMORY CYCLES:
*INNER CHILD*
*PHYSICAL*
*EMOTIONAL*
*SPIRITUAL*
AND OUR CONNECTION TO OUR INSTINCTIVE PROGRAMMING

THE SUBCONSCIOUS MIND

THIS INFORMATION IS STORED AS AN INTERCONNECTING WEB OF SENSORY EXPERIENCES

WE ARE CONDITIONED BY;
*PARENTS*
*SOCIETY*
*RELIGION*
*ROLE MODELS*
etc.

THE WAY INFORMATION IS STORED DEPENDS ON OUR CONDITIONING, PAST EXPERIENCES AND EMOTIONAL STATE AT THAT MOMENT she couldn't be far away and was most likely in the shop. It would be unusual to feel any emotion until you had gone through this analytical process. This simple example illustrates the way in which our minds assess situations as children, compared to our assessment as adults.

Hence everything that we have ever experienced, including the intensity of our emotions at the time, is stored within the subconscious mind. Situations in our adult life can trigger memories within the subconscious mind, literally making us re-experience them in the same way as we imagined the apple. However, in such cases the triggers are not deliberate.

If someone has a phobia about confined spaces for instance, something in their past has more than likely triggered this fear. It could be a result of the feeling of being trapped in a room as a small child. Although you may not be able to consciously recall this event, every time you find yourself in a confined space your conscious mind connects up with the original experience and all the fears and anxieties associated with it. This could well create an uncontrollable physical response of extreme anxiety and distress, of which there are many documented cases.

Some psychotherapy techniques, such as hypnosis, try to resolve this issue by relaxing the body and conscious mind in such a way as to enable us to recall the event in a more controlled manner. This allows our mature conscious mind to reassess the situation as an adult and this very process removes the fear and anxiety associated with the past experience. As we remove the fear and anxiety in the 'past' experience, we remove the fear and anxiety in the present and future.

If we examine the subconscious mind for a second and imagine it to be like a computer, then our memories become programmes that are stored on a moment-by-moment basis. Each memory is unique and all the emotional components associated with that memory are just as unique.

One important aspect of the subconscious mind is the child within. This inner child is a manifestation of our emotional state of being. It is in part fearful of the world, but it is also amazed at its wonder. It is in awe of every unique situation and we use its imagination to create. Our 'childlike' mind sees only endless possibilities and it is not restricted by the confines of the limited imagination of the adult. It is capable of growing and learning on a unique and high-speed level. The inner child is responsible for inventing and creating reality from within our imagination.

These elements are the positive attributes of the inner child, but it also has its negative side that is made up of the fears and distorted perceptions we accumulate due to 'childlike' immaturity. Every child will perceive everyday situations in a totally unique way. A coat hanging on a peg in a dark room, for instance, could be a monster with huge fangs, snarling and spitting fire! But a tree can be a wondrous playground, a fantasy world full of pixies and fairies.

There are always two sides to the child: one full of wonder and investigation and the other, fearful of the dark and the 'monsters' that may lurk within it. By learning how to tap into the creative, positive and special side of the inner child and allowing it to explore and grow in a positive direction, we can use its amazing creative, imaginative capabilities. In a sense, we could be an older brother or sister to it, consciously holding its hand and reassuring it when it mistakenly 'misperceives' danger and situations which can cause it to become afraid.

# THE WOUNDED, INNER CHILD

This inner child has been created through our experiences and may be understood as a unique type of 'mind cycle'. A specialised aspect of the subconscious mind has created this inner child from birth, allowing it to grow and mature to an approximate age of six. Throughout this time the subconscious will have created everything about the child - what it looks like, its visual and physical attributes, its personality, fears, hopes and dreams - based on our childhood and early life experiences.

The inner child becomes 'wounded' when it has, in a sense been 'abused', or it perceives itself as being a victim of abuse (and in some cases this is in fact so). If our childhood has been wondrous and full of love then the emotional state of our inner child is usually stable. If, however, we have had some kind of traumatic or fearful experiences as a child then these experiences may be part of our inner child which, in turn, becomes wounded by them.

It could either be the immaturity and the misperceptions of our childhood experiences that have created these wounds within our inner child, or actual experiences themselves. It makes no difference whether these experiences are real or not, because if the child within 'perceives' that it has been wounded, then it will make itself the victim.

It is the inner child's tremendous ability to create through emotion and imagination that can make it its own worse enemy. This

*HEALING THE "WOUNDED" INNER CHILD*

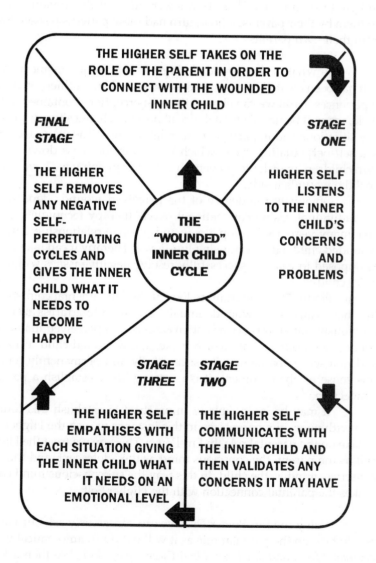

in turn can create a perceived, extreme sense of victimisation and even persecution in both the inner child and the adult.

The emotions of the wounded child have been created by a perceived inability to connect with our mother or father when we were children. Our parents, due to their own experiences as children, probably regularly used negative tactics such as manipulation through fear and guilt to control us. These tactics were most likely previously used on them by their parents, who in turn had these patterns passed down from their own parents.

So what is the wounded child? It is a unique memory cycle that has been created by our subconscious mind and influenced by our experiences. Until we can change the misperceptions contained in this cycle, we will be unable to make 'real' positive changes to our present day situations and in particular our relationships. The wounded child is a self-perpetuating cycle, which we can in fact pass down to our own children. In order to prevent this from happening we have to first heal the wounds inside.

Obviously the degree of the perceived wounds depends on the individual. Using conventional psychotherapy techniques, it can take many years to develop a new and positive relationship with the wounded child. However, using Em-Power Therapy it can take weeks as opposed to years to successfully resolve negative issues within the inner child.

Firstly, it is important to look at the fundamental components that have caused the wounds initially and then to address them. As previously stated, this cycle is often caused by a perceived inability to connect with our parents which makes the wounded child feel alone and in a sense abandoned. To successfully and permanently remove this sense of abandonment, it is necessary to re-establish a parental connection.

It may be impossible or impractical to establish this connection with your own parents, so in this instance we ask the Higher Self to take on the parental role. In Em-Power Therapy we treat the Higher Self as the parent, the conscious mind as the adolescent, and the subconscious mind as the child. In this way the subconscious mind easily makes the parental connection with the Higher Self.

Using the Em-Power Disc we can consciously ask our Higher Self to take on the parental role as it will not do so automatically. *(See diagram "The Wounded Inner Child Cycle", page 45.)* We then ask the inner child to tell the Higher Self all the things it is upset about, frightened about or feeling victimised over. In a sense, the Higher Self becomes the 'listener' and will act as a mirror for the wounded child, so that it can clarify in its own terms what all the individual issues are.

When other methods such as hypnotherapy and psychotherapy are used, often what comes out during this kind of process can be quite traumatic and painful. If it is not done correctly and under expert guidance, a person can be subjected to reliving certain situations that caused the wound in the first place, which can possibly make it worse. When using the Disc, the Higher Self will automatically 'listen and mirror', as it is not always necessary to personally or consciously experience what is actually being communicated.

The Higher Self will then talk to the inner child and from an understanding perspective will validate and affirm each situation. It gives the inner child an explanation, confirming that the situation has happened and that it makes sense given the circumstances. Then it will create all the reassurance and understanding that the inner child needs. The Higher Self empathises with each situation, providing the inner child with exactly what it needs on an emotional level to release the emotion and heal the wounds.

The Higher Self will then scan the other parts of our being to investigate whether we have anything else that is connected to, or responsible for, any aspect of our wounded child cycle. Any negative components found may be removed on our instruction. This stops the perpetuation of the wounded inner child and prevents us from projecting our misperceptions onto our own children.

Lastly, the Higher Self provides a cleansing process for the wounded child, giving it all the love that it needs on an ongoing basis. By doing this, the wounded child not only becomes healthy, but it also stops being a negative trigger in the subconscious mind. It will become an everlasting source of joy and inspiration, rather than a catalyst for guilt, fear and negative experience.

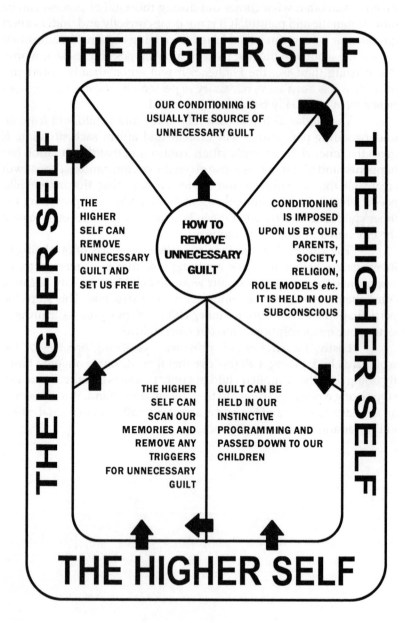

# THE GUILT TRIP

Strange as it might seem, guilt appears to be a sought out and highly prized emotion within most people's day-to-day lives. Many parents find guilt the only method upon which to control the actions of their mischievous children. This is not usually their fault however, as they were most probably subjected to guilt by their own parents.

Eventually, over generations, guilt-driven control can actually be impregnated into our instinctive programming, making us even more susceptible to these feelings. If we were fed guilt as a child in the same way we were fed milk, over time we naturally start to expect it, especially from our parents. It is as if it becomes a comforter. In later life, in our search to fill the void that appears when we leave home, we even find partners who continually use guilt. Unfortunately guilt is available in abundance, whenever we need it! Not everyone uses guilt in this way, however, and when we do come across someone who is guilt-free they almost seem too good to be true.

Guilt is an addiction for many people and it could be the basis for most addictions from alcohol to drugs, cigarettes and food. There is an element of guilt in every type of addictive behaviour. Unnecessary guilt is a piece of baggage that we carry around with us all the time to the extent that we feel we would be lost without it.

Hence we have to look at the emotion of guilt in more depth and attempt to analyse why we have this incessant need to have it in our everyday lives. Guilt is almost certainly part of our instinctive programming and it was perhaps originally intended as an emotional aspect of our conscience, helping us discriminate between right and wrong.

Our social and cultural backgrounds impose a set of rules upon us so that we become conditioned in one way or another to certain generalised viewpoints. If a situation occurs when the rules appear to be broken, guilt sets in to bring us back in line with our conscience.

It is our conditioning that is really directly responsible for the extent, and our experience of, guilt. We adopt values and beliefs from our parents, family, school and peers. Particularly if there has been a breakdown in the relationship at home, we will turn to outside influences and role models. These may include pop stars, footballers and actors as well as the messages from advertising and marketing. Often this conditioning comes through very positive means and, for example, may take the form of perceived love.

A child loves his or her parents and wants to be loved by

them. The same will also apply to any role model. If we are in love then we will often do anything to keep that love, even if this involves giving 'something' of ourselves. As teenagers we will go out and buy the records of our favourite pop star, for instance, because we love the artist. The more we play their records then the more loved we will feel in return.

All media communication processes (music, films, advertising, news, etc), involve a kind of conditioning to some degree. One reason we enjoy a film is because it will either conflict or agree with our conditioning. Violent films or horror films generate a certain emotion inside us because they go against what we believe to be right. Horror films and the concepts of monsters, vampires and werewolves trigger our survival instincts, spontaneously producing adrenaline in the body and creating a rush of excitement. Certain comedians can recreate uncomfortable situations that may conflict with, or are even a part of, our conditioning. Either way, their jokes are easily recognisable and will make us chuckle. Additionally, clever marketing companies manipulate our emotions to literally get us to do anything.
Only by understanding why we respond in a certain way do we gain the ability to set ourselves free from any conditioning, intentional or otherwise, that others are trying to impose upon us.

On a physical and practical level and in relation to self-healing, the Em-Power Healing System is specifically designed to give the individual control and to increase our ability to understand ourselves. It is far better to be able to individually decide on what conditioning we would prefer to have imposed upon us. For example, if it is your wish to become more spiritually minded, then conditioning which would help you realise that goal would be of great value. This may take the form of various types of philosophies, which you might consider to be positive and good. Hence the whole learning process involves conditioning and you should consciously decide on a personal level what is best for you. *(See diagram "Removal of Unnecessary Guilt", page 48).*

The part of us that perpetuates a negative condition is the subconscious mind, as this is the sum of all our experiences. All negative conditioning is stored in the subconscious and this can lead us down the path of self-destruction. The only part of our being that truly knows which kind of conditioning is best for us is the Higher Self.
Through communication with the Higher Self we can discover what forms of conditioning are going to be beneficial. On a purely personal level I used to like to watch a good horror movie, but accord-

ing to my Higher Self this wasn't particularly beneficial for me. After asking why this was the case, it came into my awareness that a constant subjection to acts of violence was only serving to anaesthetise my conscience into accepting even more violence. In other words, the more I saw, the more acceptable or normal it appeared to be. This may be different for you and you would have to ask your Higher Self what kind of things would be beneficial for you over a long term basis. It is possible to do this using Em-Power Therapy.

## HOW TO BREAK AWAY FROM OUR CONDITIONING AND REMOVE UNNECESSARY GUILT.

Firstly, it is very important to mention that some forms of guilt are entirely necessary and valuable because they form part of our conscience and help us to live in society. We are not suggesting that we remove or try to adjust this necessary guilt. On the contrary, it is the intention here to improve the conscience, to help distinguish correctly between what is right and wrong.

### *EMOTIONAL GUILT*

We also need to be aware that guilt exists on all levels: emotional, spiritual and physical. Perhaps the form of guilt that we are most aware of is the emotional - the guilt imposed by others or ourselves, that we negatively feed upon. We are often unaware of emotional guilt at the time it is being formed and it is only afterwards, when we are able to analyse a situation, that we realise guilt is what we are feeling. In addition, on an emotional level, we need to ensure that other people do not impose unnecessary guilt upon us. Here, we would use the Em-Power Disc to enable us to connect to the Higher Self and ask it to allow us to perceive every situation accurately so that we can respond in the appropriate way. This would allow a person who perhaps has been numbed or influenced by improper conditioning to break away and go back to a conscious moral sense of right and wrong.

## *PHYSICAL AND SPIRITUAL GUILT*

Guilt can also affect us by manifesting on a physical level. It can create common symptoms such as backache, neck problems, tension and arthritic conditions. It can also develop into a negative emotional 'programme' which perpetuates an ongoing cycle affecting us on a physical and emotional level. Physical guilt always has an emotional component and we must look at the emotional aspects before we try to heal the physical problems.

Most formal religions attempt to impose spiritual guilt and conditioning to try to make the individual follow a specific ideology. This is not necessarily a bad thing if the ultimate goal is positive, but we need to be aware of this attempted imposition. At the end of the day, we must all decide for ourselves whether it is appropriate for this kind of spiritual guilt to be imposed upon us and whether it serves any useful purpose.

Guilt often stimulates a kind of two-way conversation inside our minds, which we will consider next.

# INTERNAL DIALOGUE

We all have a communication process that takes place within our conscious minds on a moment-by-moment basis. We call this conversation our 'Internal Dialogue', and it is the way in which we talk to ourselves, as we constantly analyse our lives.

As the information we receive is often incomplete, our internal dialogue will assess it, compare and interpret it using information gained from our experiences stored in the subconscious mind, and then make various assumptions. For example, imagine yourself going to the dentist for a check-up. Depending on your past experiences many things will go through your mind as it is a situation where the outcome is uncertain. We effortlessly use our imagination to fill in the blanks either correctly or incorrectly, depending on our personality and our emotional and physical state of being at that precise moment. As they sit in the waiting room, one person might think they need at least twenty fillings. They may focus on the pain of the injection and even perhaps experience anxiety and stress. Another person may analyse the situation in a completely different way, perhaps assuming that because they haven't had any dental problems in the past, they won't need any treatment at all. They might therefore feel completely relaxed about it!

Internal dialogue is a key to directing our lives in a more positive way if we can learn how to control it properly. However, there are certain rules that apply when we have this personal conversation.

The consequences of internal dialogue can affect us on all levels - emotional, physical, mental and spiritual. We may not always be aware of it, but we emotionally assess and experience each second. As our emotional states are recorded, analysed and interpreted, our conscious and subconscious minds send subtle messages around the body altering our state of being on a moment by moment basis. *(See diagram "Internal Dialogue", page 54).*

For example, it is easy to say to yourself "I feel sick", or "I feel tired". Although we may not verbalise these statements, our bodies are nevertheless listening and responding to each and every aspect of our internal communication.

Becoming aware of our internal dialogue can be very self-empowering when we realise that we often say things to ourselves that we don't really mean. Even though we are often not aware we are doing this, it is easy to develop particular negative habits of communicating with ourselves. Although this may not have any major effect in the short term, it can have a severe effect in the long term.

*INTERNAL DIALOGUE*

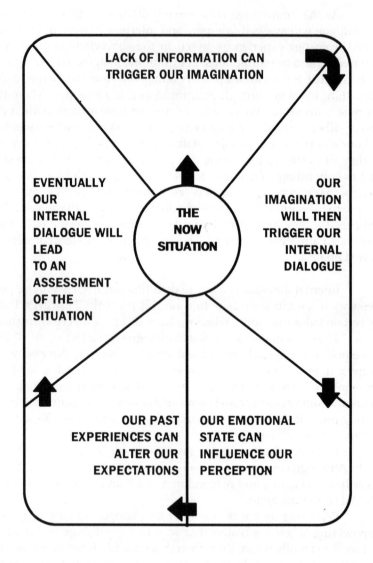

Put yourself in the following situation. You have agreed to meet a special person for a date, and they are late. Depending on your personality and past experiences and how well you know the person, it is easy to construct in your mind a lot of different scenarios to justify and explain to yourself why they haven't arrived. This could be anything from... "They don't want to see me", "They've had an accident", "They can't be bothered", "I'm not good enough for them", or "They don't think they're good enough for me".

However ridiculous this kind of reasoning may appear, your present state of mind will affect how you think. In addition, what has happened to you a few minutes earlier will dictate how you are feeling. If you are in a positive frame of mind it is easier to construct an internal dialogue which will give the person who's late the benefit of the doubt. If you're in a negative frame of mind then you'll concoct a whole pot of deception, which can lead to paranoia.

Our internal dialogue is a natural process and it is necessary for our survival, as it is the basis from which we decide on a course of action. It is important to interpret information correctly and to remember that it is usually our emotional state that will guide us, possibly diverting our analytical process and sometimes misinterpreting situations.

A balanced emotional state allows you to better assess your position. Recognising the part that emotion is playing in your internal dialogue will empower you and help you to understand the situation for what it is, rather than allowing your imagination to get the better of you.

# DEFINING OUR EMOTIONS

In any given situation, we can misinterpret information depending on our mood state. Let's look at the basic emotions that could cause this. There are perhaps four fundamental emotional states - happy, sad, scared and angry, which can generate feelings such as insecurity, envy, greed, fear, hate, joy, love, jealousy and indifference.

## *NEGATIVE EMOTION*

We believe that a balanced emotional state is the key to rational internal dialogue. If this is so then we can waste a lot of mental energy by indulging ourselves in negative emotional dialogue.

Here are some words that may trigger internal dialogue:

*Boyfriend/girlfriend*
*Job interview*
*Mother/father*
*Terrorist threat*
*Illness (yourself or a loved one)*
*Cancer*
*Holidays*
*Moving house*
*Paradise*
*Divorce*
*Winning the lottery*
*Wedding (marriage)*
*Sex*

To identify negative emotion and put it into perspective, try the following exercises:

## *TRIGGERS FOR INTERNAL DIALOGUE*

### Exercise 1.

In this exercise, you could pick three of the above and as you think about them, write a list of all the things that go through your mind. As an experiment, you could ask someone else to think of the same three things and compare the difference between their internal dialogue and your own.

## Exercise 2.

Think of a situation that would make you envious. It could be someone you work closely with, who you like and admire. Let's say they receive a promotion instead of you. How does this make you feel? You know that this person is well qualified and well deserving of the promotion - however, so are you. Think about your feelings in this situation and what thoughts and internal dialogue go through your mind!

## Exercise 3.

Imagine a situation that would make you experience a feeling of greed. For example, someone is prepared to give you as much as you want of something, but you decide to take more than you actually need. Greed is wanting something over and above what you need. If it's food, then you eat for the sake of eating - because it's there. Or in a relationship, we may unnecessarily take advantage of a situation. We can often justify or make excuses for being greedy, as it is usually associated with material possession and having more of something can make us feel more secure.

## Exercise 4.

Think of a situation that would frighten you such as flying or heights. Fear is an extreme feeling of not being in control. We can also experience fear due to a loss of some kind - anything from the loss of trust in a person to the death of a loved one.

## Exercise 5.

Now think of a situation where you would feel hatred. This is when you want something negative to happen to someone else, and could be due to a combination of fear and jealousy. For example, if someone injured or maimed a member of your family, was responsible for putting someone close to you in danger, or was deliberately depriving you of something you really needed, you may experience feelings of hatred. Many people hate themselves or parts of themselves.

## Exercise 6.

Think of a situation where you could feel jealousy or envy. Extreme jealousy or envy is purely personal in that it is a different experience for everyone. It is when you want something that someone else has, simply because they have it.

## Exercise 7.

Imagine feeling indifferent. Indifference is a lack of concern for a person, situation or thing. If you are indifferent to something, then it has no meaning or influence over you, and you don't care.

## Exercise 8.

Put yourself into a situation where you would feel angry. Anger is a feeling of extreme hostility, indignation, exasperation and rage. It is when you perceive situations, events, people and circumstances to conflict with your personal interests and be beyond your control.

## *POSITIVE EMOTION*

Now let's look at some positive emotions. Caring is when our attention or focus is directed towards another on an emotional, physical and spiritual level. Our degree of caring determines our action. If a physical action (such as a war or famine) conflicts with our sense of morality then we label it 'caring'. Many people are not spurred into action because they feel guilty, but if they care and feel guilty at the same time then they may do something positive about it. Compassion is caring that is not driven by guilt. It is fairly instinctive but also possible to attain as we develop respect for others.

The act of feeling in love is a perceived extreme emotional need to a point where the well being of the focus of the love is more important than our personal integrity, survival or wants. It is an all-consuming, intense, emotional need.

Real love, in all probability, cannot be completely defined but let's look at what many people experience as love. It involves mutual respect and admiration and a fusing together of two people to the point where existence feels inappropriate without the other. If this feeling isn't continuously totally mutual, then love may cease to exist for a person. However, I personally believe that true love is a feeling of oneness with the 'source of our existence'. It is an emanation of pure joy that exists in a place within each of us.

In summary, if we can learn to define our emotions, we can more easily identify them as we are experiencing them. But the negative internal dialogue must be neutralised and replaced with positive internal dialogue. Using Em-Power Therapy we learn how to automatically activate this conversion process, creating balance and harmony within the body and mind. We can learn how to release emotions of joy, serenity and peace without feeling guilty about it!

# POSITIVE AND NEGATIVE IMAGINATION

*"The computer is merely a simplified physical manifestation of that which already exists within each of us..."*

We human beings have strived to make our environment reflect our inner minds. We have done this by using our imagination to create that which exists within the boundaries of present day understanding. In other words, if we can conceptualise something, no matter how far fetched and if we are determined enough and resourceful enough, it will only be a matter of time before we achieve that dream.

An example of this is landing on the moon. A hundred years ago, sending a space craft to the moon would have sounded ludicrous to most people. But if one person can dream up such an idea, then eventually others will have the same idea or share the same goals and find a way to accomplish them.

As we create and expand our mental and physical boundaries an interesting thing happens: instead of using up good ideas, one idea often leads to another. First of all there is imagination and then through the act of creation we often go beyond the original thought to a new level of heightened awareness, to a new idea that was brought to light because of the first one. Take Edison for example. He imagined what it would be like if he could light up our streets and homes and eventually he discovered a way of doing it. Subsequently other inventors used the basis of his original idea by taking electricity as a power source to run appliances at home and at work. If Edison had not laid the foundation by making electricity readily available, others would perhaps never have thought of the television! Without the electricity to run these devices, they would never have been thought about.

So many future ideas and concepts may probably sound like science fiction at the moment, but we should remember that none of our past great achievements could have happened without the idea in the first place.

Over the centuries, human kind has always looked to that which already exists in nature for their inspiration. We have often tried to reproduce nature for personal benefit. For example the idea for aircraft design was probably the bird, and fish and aquatic life for the submarine. Necessity has often been the mother and father of invention. Events such as war and the pursuit of better ways to kill each other have been the catalyst for most of the twentieth century's inventions. This may be a very cynical view and we must not forget that there have been some exceptionally good ideas, which have made life on the whole much easier. But it all depends on how you look at it.

A plane can be used to take you to a faraway destination for the holiday of a lifetime, or it can drop a bomb on thousands of unsuspecting civilians. The idea of the aeroplane has revolutionised transportation and communication around the world, but is it a good or bad thing? Really, it is what we do with these inventions that's good or bad and the choice has always been ours.

The forces used in a bomb could be harnessed to provide light and heat for people who are cold. Chemical warfare could be redirected into the pursuit of new ways to feed the starving millions. But until we can learn to control our negative imagination we will always find ways to destroy and maim, scarring the lives, hearts and minds of generations to come.

The key to the world's ills does not exist on the outside (i.e. the physical world), but can be found on the inside in the world of our imagination, or spiritual world. If we change our negative imagination to positive imagination we can create a world that everyone can be proud to be a part of. A few people trying to save the world by throwing themselves in front of a train carrying nuclear waste for example, will be crushed, if not by the train, then by those who protect the train. I am suggesting that fragmented pockets of people with positive views and ideologies will be unable to stem the tide of the masses. It is only by improving our awareness of the consequences of specific actions that we can hope to resolve issues on a global scale. Unfortunately, in this world we have created for ourselves, negative imagination is poisoning society and destroying the very foundation of goodness that is positive imagination.

The reason we talk about negative and positive imagination is to put across the magnitude of the task that lies ahead for everybody. If we cannot learn to control this force that exists within us and use it positively, (on a planetary scale), we could be swept away in a tide of destruction.

Technology is now at a point where our worst negative thoughts can come true. (In the context of the Em-Power Disc, fortunately, negative imagination has no power, as our thoughts do not form a language that the Higher Self will act upon. This means that if we think in a negative way it will not have a detrimental effect because out thoughts are not constructed in a way that the Higher Self will understand while wearing the Disc).

Normally our negative imagination can have a detrimental physical, emotional or spiritual effect. If a thought, idea or concept - negative or positive - is repeated often enough, at some point the subconscious mind (which cannot tell the difference between imagination and reality) will eventually take this concept on board. Therefore this idea could have a detrimental effect both in the present and in the future. Further, the idea will remain unchanged unless we replace it with new positive imagination to neutralise the effects of the original negative thought. The Em-Power Disc can help us control any unintentional thought processes that may affect us on a negative level. It gives us a kind of buffer zone of time so that we can clarify the kinds of thought processes that we would like our subconscious mind to store. The principle is similar to that of the 'spell check' on a computer, allowing you to take a look at what you have written for the purpose of clarification before you make a decision to 'save' it.

Memories with high emotional content are easier to remember than ones without. Survival, the most basic of all instincts, will often spontaneously trigger physical responses in some situations. This can release endorphins and adrenaline, your natural pain killing and energy boosting drugs, into your body. In extreme circumstances these responses could be inappropriate and lead to action that you might regret later. Negative imagination can often trigger improper and badly timed responses that may be self-destructive or could even escalate into an uncontrollable response endangering the people closest to you.

Knowing how and why these things happen is the first step. We will now look at the concept of negative and positive imagination and how we can redirect our thoughts in order to best control our lives.

## NEGATIVE IMAGINATION.

Negative imagination usually stems from a sense of perceived danger or loss. This creates fear, which then stimulates the senses with adrenaline thus heightening our false perception. When this happens, our negative imagination will run riot. As it grows it is self-fuelling. The body releases natural chemicals that stimulate the mind and other parts of the body, thereby creating more tension. Sometimes the release of these natural chemicals can totally inhibit logical thinking and make a person extremely aggressive to the point where they may become violent or they may even attempt to injure another, possibly without realising it. It is not until the reaction has subsided that their conscious logical mind regains control of their body. A typical example is found in some marital domestic situations, where one partner becomes violent towards the other and is largely unaware of their actions. For short periods of time the other person will become the focus of uncontrollable rage. The violent person can also become stronger due to the introduction of adrenaline into the system.

Negative imagination restricts the natural communication processes in the body and mind and, if maintained, can actually cause damage to many systems within the body. Negative imagination can often be a result of past situations contained within our subconscious. As events unfold, they can trigger these associated feelings which may not be relevant in the present but serve to stimulate and support our current frame of mind. As similar thoughts attract each other through the subconscious law of attraction, our minds bring together all these past events and allow them to fuel and stimulate our emotions.

A negative event will always plant a seed, which could either bring about a positive change or perpetuate more negative events. If we develop a level of caring or compassion somewhere along life's road, then the seed will grow into positive change. The compassion in itself can actually change the polarity from negative creating a positive shift.

Think of an event from the past that was negative due to your own thought processes or actions. An example might be not allowing another child to join in with your group of friends at school. At that time you may have thought that the other child was too young and immature, as this would have been happening around the age when you were trying to act grown-up. Later, as you developed compassion, you would instinctively realise that this action of exclusion was unjustified, and should similar sets of circumstances re-occur you wouldn't respond in the same way.

## POSITIVE IMAGINATION

Positive imagination can not only help you to have an optimistic view of life, but it can inspire you to achieve your goals. A positive and vivid imagination can be a powerful ally when others may be floundering in self-pity. The ability to use positive imagination can have a profound effect over everything we do, literally making anything possible. Well directed positive imagination can summon up the power of the universe, it is the stuff of genius that can allow us to fulfil our destiny. Positive imagination is the key to accessing universal healing energy, the pure 'godly' energy that is available to everyone. By simply asking for what we want through communication with the Higher Self, we can make it appear or become available to us. Positive imagination can help us to achieve all this and much more. Ideas can shape the world as the good of all mankind exists within us and if we learn to access this information we can make our lives more meaningful.

# THE LAWS AND PRINCIPLES OF IMAGINATION

*Your actions reflect your beliefs.*
*Beliefs become your reality.*
*A conceptual thought becomes reality.*
*Control imagination and control your life.*
*Fear is a perceived lack of control.*
*Your perception of the outside world is a reflection of your inner world.*
*Positive change equals positive imagination.*
*You receive what you expect, not what you want.*
*Emotional 'baggage' produces negative reactions.*
*Absence of direction leads to stagnation.*
*Whatever you give freely you shall receive easily.*
*Whatever you take forcefully is not real.*
*Imagination, negative or positive, is like a seed that grows through stimulation.*
*An imagination that lacks stimulation dies.*
*Knowledge of the laws of imagination brings forth understanding.*

# HOW DO WE CHANGE NEGATIVE IMAGINATION INTO POSITIVE IMAGINATION?

In order to convert negative into positive imagination, we must change the habits of our negative mind-set and this can be achieved in a number of ways. In hypnotherapy, for instance, the therapist may try to show you a way of communicating with the subconscious mind to try to facilitate a change on a subconscious level. This is done by persuading the subconscious that there is no perceived benefit for the individual to continue with the same old negative programme. As previously stated, the subconscious mind acts like a six-year-old child and therefore must be persuaded skilfully. If the therapist is successful, the subconscious will filter the message to the Higher Self, which will take it on board and adjust the person's mind-set accordingly. This is a very successful process in many cases, but only if the person in question wants to make significant changes. However, while hypnosis is a possible approach, you may not be the kind of person that can be easily hypnotised.

Negative imagination can be part of our instinctive programming in that it may be inherited and also may be present in other members of the family. Instinctive programming is very difficult to alter using hypnosis as it is not contained within our subconscious mind, although we may be able to recall events and situations where our negative programming has played a significant part in causing friction and creating unnecessary distress to ourselves and others. Since the only aspect of our mind capable of adjusting instinctive programming is the Higher Self, talking to the subconscious mind would not be appropriate in this particular case - we need to talk directly to the Higher Self to be able to achieve long-lasting results.

The degree to which our Higher Self responds is directly related to how much we really want to make positive changes. It is also determined by how our Higher Self interprets our commands and the directions we give it.

It is very important that we believe in our Higher Self's ability to act on our behalf for our highest good and enable us to change negative programming to positive. The key to change is the belief and trust in one's own Higher Self. The only way we can increase our belief in the existence of the Higher Self is with practical, physical proof. Em-Power Therapy gives the proof we need to intensify our faith in our own Higher Self, as it works beyond any belief system.

If we believe in our Higher Self one hundred percent and ask it to do something, however difficult or illogical, provided it is for our highest good, it will achieve a hundred percent of our initial goal. If we only believe in our Higher Self fifty percent, then we may only be able to achieve half our goal. This particularly applies to non-physical commands such as anything emotional and definitely applies to any severe physical illness.

Hence Em-Power Therapy is designed to alter our negative imagination to positive imagination by using the Em-Power Disc. Basically, we tell the Higher Self to remove any negative emotional, physical or spiritual influence and replace it with the positive. The Higher Self also tells our body and mind at every level to remove all negative energy and replace it with positive energy.

As far as the body and mind are concerned, the words 'energy' and 'thinking' are similar. It's almost like saying the same thing. In fact using the word 'energy' is possibly better than using the word 'thinking', because it deals with all aspects of one's being on all levels. Many people's Higher Self communication processes are very literal and the word 'thinking' could be interpreted to mean just the mental process.

# INSTINCTIVE PROGRAMMING

We have already likened instinctive programming to DNA, 'the building blocks of life'. DNA determines the characteristics of our entire being - physical, mental, emotional and perhaps even spiritual. We are born with a combination of our mother and father's DNA and this is an ancestral line that can go back for thousands, perhaps even millions, of years. In other words, evolution and the random coming together of individuals through the act of procreation have determined who we are. All the good things and all the bad things are recorded within our DNA. Instinctive programming can be described in a similar way.

Every aspect of our DNA structure, all the genetic codes determining our emotional and physical make-up and our entire ancestral and cultural heritage, exists in some form within our instinctive programming. Instinctive programming explains, in simple terms, the mystical and mysterious abilities that we all possess. In the same way that the coming together of different chemicals create different chemical reactions, the coming together of individuals will create new and unique human beings. These beings will have both similarities to and dramatic differences from their predecessors, arising from their unique physical, mental and emotional attributes.

Imagine a village or a community that has been isolated from the rest of the world. You would find that although there have been subtle changes in the lives of that community, drastic changes would not have occurred unless there was some kind of external influence. Such external influences would include contact with other cultures, climatic changes and unpredicted calamities such as drought, famine, flood or earthquake.

Unless there is an upheaval in the village's way of life, the social structure, attitudes of the people and general physical characteristics will remain the same. Good examples of this are the isolated tribes in the rain forests whose existence has remained unchanged for probably thousands of years, until discovered by modern day explorers. It is known that entire tribes have been wiped out by something as simple as a common cold, introduced into their community by 'outsiders'. The results have been catastrophic, as their immune systems have never had to fight such viruses before.

As our world grows smaller due to the advances in communication, transport and technology, our instinctive programming changes more rapidly. We are prone to thinking differently since our

*INSTINCTIVE PROGRAMMING AND OUR*
*INHERITED ATTRIBUTES*

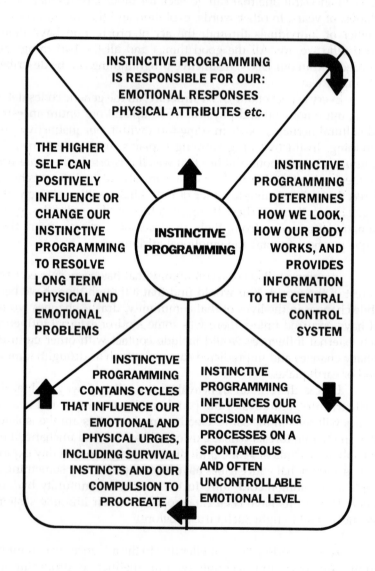

cultures are rapidly opening up to influences, beliefs and concepts from around the world. In most ways this is a good thing as it brings together people that were once restricted by their environment, thinking and cultures.

Let's look at instinctive programming in simple terms *(See Diagram "Instinctive Programming and our Inherited Attributes", page 66).* Every person included in your family tree has contributed throughout the generations to shape and form your instinctive programming, making you the person that you are today. The vastness of our instinctive programming is overwhelming and it can explain many of our beliefs and emotional responses. Our instinctive programming is made up of numerous parts, but the main ones that can influence us in our daily lives are: physical attributes, emotional states, spiritual awareness, inherited thinking, rigidity of thought, the ability to adjust to one's surroundings, the ability to absorb new information, sexual responses and survival instincts.

Included within the instinctive programming are the actual 'blueprints' for life and the technical information of our existence. It houses evolutionary information which one day may be triggered and would not only set mankind on a new evolutionary path, but probably change the very fabric of the universe as we know it.

*THE CENTRAL CONTROL SYSTEM*

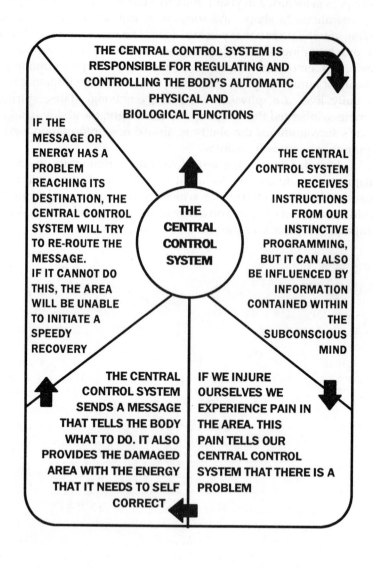

THE CENTRAL CONTROL SYSTEM IS RESPONSIBLE FOR REGULATING AND CONTROLLING THE BODY'S AUTOMATIC PHYSICAL AND BIOLOGICAL FUNCTIONS

IF THE MESSAGE OR ENERGY HAS A PROBLEM REACHING ITS DESTINATION, THE CENTRAL CONTROL SYSTEM WILL TRY TO RE-ROUTE THE MESSAGE. IF IT CANNOT DO THIS, THE AREA WILL BE UNABLE TO INITIATE A SPEEDY RECOVERY

THE CENTRAL CONTROL SYSTEM

THE CENTRAL CONTROL SYSTEM RECEIVES INSTRUCTIONS FROM OUR INSTINCTIVE PROGRAMMING, BUT IT CAN ALSO BE INFLUENCED BY INFORMATION CONTAINED WITHIN THE SUBCONSCIOUS MIND

THE CENTRAL CONTROL SYSTEM SENDS A MESSAGE THAT TELLS THE BODY WHAT TO DO. IT ALSO PROVIDES THE DAMAGED AREA WITH THE ENERGY THAT IT NEEDS TO SELF CORRECT

IF WE INJURE OURSELVES WE EXPERIENCE PAIN IN THE AREA. THIS PAIN TELLS OUR CENTRAL CONTROL SYSTEM THAT THERE IS A PROBLEM

# THE CENTRAL CONTROL SYSTEM

The central control system is believed to be a type of master control mechanism that is responsible for all the automatic and inherent processes within the body. The central control system is the link between the body and mind.

There are nine known systems in the body and each one is responsible for maintaining balance and regulating a specific function (this is known as homeostasis).

Most doctors and therapists agree that the body is more than just a collection of separate systems that regulate themselves. Rather, each system is connected and forms an integral part of a complete sophisticated mechanism. The word 'holistic' means treating the body as a whole and even conventional medicine now agrees with this approach in principle.

The central control system regulates and integrates each system, instructing it to work as a whole, sending messages from the brain via the central nervous system. The Em-Power Healing System, in conjunction with the Em-Power Disc, can intensify our control and provide us with the ability to communicate on a totally unique level with the brain and the central control system. *(See diagram "The Central Control System", page 68).*

Electrical impulses containing messages and instructions to parts of our body travel through what are commonly known as 'meridians' or energy channels. These channels form very complex communication pathways within the body. The ancient technique of acupuncture uses needles that are designed to release any blockages that may exist within these communication pathways, so allowing the correct messages to reach their designated point. If a blockage exists, the central control system attempts to release it by either sending more energy to the blockage or re-routing the communication signals through the surrounding area, thus by-passing the blockage altogether and allowing the energy to reach its destination.

## THE CENTRAL CONTROL SYSTEM AND PAIN

Pain is an indicator, or marker, within the body, which tells us something is wrong. It has an important and necessary function. When we are injured we experience pain at the point of injury. The pain itself acts as a trigger causing a chain reaction within the body, telling the central control system that there is a problem in this specific area. The central control system in turn, sends energy towards the co-ordinates or location indicated by the pain.

When pain is a result of a blockage of some kind within the body, the energy being sent from the central control system can either not reach the location of the injury or the amount of energy is greatly reduced. This slows down the healing process and the effect is similar to having a partly charged battery inside an electronic toy. If this happens, then the body will lose its power and literally run itself down, finding it difficult to heal itself. In this situation the central control system may try to re-route energy around the blockage in an attempt to 'build a bridge' and thus allow the energy to be diverted. Eventually, the energy will reach its destination, letting the body heal itself.

Alternatively the central control system will increase the energy flow in an attempt to 'blast' its way through the blockage itself. This is why in healing, as a blockage is being removed, a patient can often feel tremendous heat which appears to be coming from the hands of the healer. However the temperature of the hands of the healer will not have changed.

Sometimes the central control system is unable to by-pass the blockage and subsequently a malfunction, such as a physical swelling or pain occurs. This problem exists because the healing process requires sufficient energy and if the energy is slowed down or stops, so does the healing. In order to correct such a physical problem, we must find a way of reconnecting or releasing this stubborn energy blockage. Many people find that the Em-Power Disc helps them to do this because it intensifies the flow of energy to the blockage.

By using very simple unblocking techniques, you can place the Disc on the area and release the blockage. By allowing the correct amount of healing energy to reach the problem area, it will then spontaneously self-correct. So, in actuality, in this respect the Em-Power Disc is a bit like an amplifier on a stereo system. It offers us the ability to adjust the volume and the quality of the sound coming from the speakers.

It would be foolish to use the Em-Power Disc to merely 'mask' pain, however. Imagine that someone broke their leg, then immediately told their body to remove the pain and it did so. If that person continued to walk around on this broken leg, they could cause massive long-term and perhaps even irreparable damage.

It concerns me when I watch some healers asking people in wheelchairs who are unable to walk to use their 'faith' to get up out of the chair and take a few steps. If an individual is 'whipped up' into an emotional frenzy their adrenaline levels can be so high that pain can disappear in the short term in some instances, and perhaps a person could feel able to stand up and walk. If encouraged to do so, this action can potentially cause more long-term damage, not only on a physical level but on a psychological one, as disappointment will inevitably set in when the adrenaline levels drop later and the pain returns. We must always, therefore, deal with the symptoms and the cause of the pain.

I recommend that if someone is experiencing pain of any kind they should always see a doctor and allow them to diagnose the problem and prescribe the appropriate medication. If, however, medication is purely designed to remove pain, you could use the Em-Power Disc if you preferred. On the other hand, if a drug is designed to have a therapeutic function and is part of the healing process itself, then I would strongly advise continuation of medication and use of the Disc in conjunction, to help speed up the process. We need to apply common sense in such matters.

We can tell the central control system to reduce the level of pain. Often the degree of pain will be lowered as the healing energy starts to self-correct the area. Although the Em-Power Disc in many cases can help to reduce the level of pain, it is more important to use it to trigger a process which will attempt to identify, and correct, the cause of a specific problem, to ensure the pain does not return.

For example, if I have a tooth that needs filling, I would use the Disc to help remove or reduce my level of pain until I could get an appointment with my dentist. In this particular case the Disc is useful as a temporary measure. But if I had a lower back problem, or a frozen shoulder, I would need to communicate with my central control system, via the Higher Self, and tell it to give me what I needed to remove and correct the symptoms and the cause of this specific problem. The central control system will do whatever is necessary to try and self-correct, balance and normalise any specific problem that may occur, and it will do this by using all means available to it. Often during a correction process using Em-Power Therapy the body will move spontaneously or it will self-manipulate in order to achieve the desired result.

The central control system, in conjunction with the brain, controls and regulates what can be described as instinctive and spontaneous pre-programmed responses to given situations. Such responses might be anything from a knee-jerk reaction due to the stimulation of certain nerves, to the sudden release of pain signals when you burn yourself, where you will automatically pull your hand away. On a more sophisticated level, the central control system controls, regulates and integrates all the automatic and biological functions within the body.

The access point for the central control system in relation to Em-Power Therapy is located in the nape of the neck, the link between the brain and the physical body. If a blockage occurs around this area, it can cause many problems throughout the entire body including low immune systems, low energy levels, chronic fatigue and muscle wasting. When the Em-Power Disc is placed at the access point, it can release the blockage and may trigger spontaneous movement such as an arm lifting.

It is my belief that the brain is an organism responsible for housing our consciousness, although our consciousness extends beyond the physical body. It is the brain that allows our consciousness to communicate with our physical body. The physical body in turn allows the consciousness to experience life through our physical senses. Thus the brain is like a control centre for a vast communications network. Memories, thoughts and the entire communication process within the body are a result of our consciousness manipulating what I call 'intelligent biological energies'. This intelligent energy stores our consciousness and physical programming within complex and elaborate energy formations that are similar to electromagnetic fields.

When we use the Em-Power Disc to communicate with the central control system, our consciousness in conjunction with all aspects of our being often constructs extremely sophisticated biophysical responses in order to complete whatever task we have consciously decided to set ourselves.

# THE HIGHER SELF

*(See diagram "The Higher Self", page 74)*

The most remarkable and amazing aspect of human consciousness is called the Higher Self, which is a benevolent intelligence we all possess and represents human potential. The Higher Self is our 'spiritual' self.

Throughout human evolution and development, mankind has perceived itself to be more than just a 'physical' body and many philosophies and religions believe in the concept of the spiritual self or soul. Investigation into this subject, however, has been very limited and left to the realms of the 'paranormal' or 'mystical'. By incorporating the Em-Power Healing System into daily life, it is possible for an individual to develop a relationship with their Higher Self. The entire function and purpose of the Higher Self is to help us achieve our goals and serve as our guide and conscience through life. Em-Power Therapy can completely remove any doubts that you may have about merely being a physical body.

In order to communicate with any form of intelligence we would first have to develop basic communication skills and a rudimentary language. It is helpful here to draw a comparison between communicating with the Higher Self and talking to a computer. A computer will only respond if we ask questions in the right way; similar rules apply to communication with the Higher Self.

The Em-Power Disc gives our conscious mind the ability to communicate with our Higher Self, giving us access to unlimited potential. Above and beyond the Higher Self lies the Human Group Consciousness, the thread that links all mankind. Beyond that is the Universal Mind, that which links all things together. The Higher Self is the only part of our being that is capable and sophisticated enough to access the Human Group Consciousness and the Universal Mind. (See diagram "The Interactive Mind Model", page 76).

When we activate the Em-Power Disc, our goal is to make a connection to the Higher Self. In the next section we will now look at this connection in detail and answer some of the most commonly asked questions.

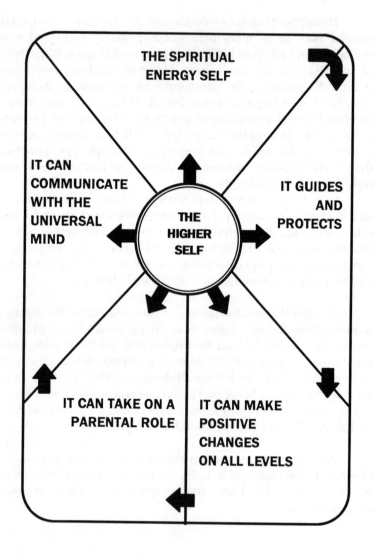

THE SPIRITUAL
ENERGY SELF

IT CAN
COMMUNICATE
WITH THE
UNIVERSAL
MIND

THE
HIGHER
SELF

IT GUIDES
AND
PROTECTS

IT CAN TAKE ON A
PARENTAL ROLE

IT CAN MAKE
POSITIVE
CHANGES
ON ALL LEVELS

*"THE HIGHER SELF IS A BENEVOLENT
INTELLIGENCE THAT WE ALL POSSESS"*

# WHAT IS HIGHER SELF COMMUNICATION?

It is the ability to communicate with our 'spirit' or 'energy' self. By making this connection we can access an intellect that is beyond our experience, our conscious understanding and present day knowledge. The Higher Self's primary function is to evolve us, but it can only do this if we are aware of it and ready and able to listen.

We believe that a full Higher Self connection may be the next step in human evolution. As previously stated, the Higher Self is in a sense like a mature adult or parent, while the conscious mind is like an adolescent and the subconscious mind is like a child. They are all quite separate but nevertheless inexplicably linked on an interdependence. It is important to recognise each part to fully understand how they fit together in the grand scheme of things.

The ultimate goal of any intelligence is to fulfil its true potential. Therefore, as individuals, our goal should be to allow these three aspects of ourselves to 'merge' together for our greatest good.

The Em-Power Healing System is designed to make it possible for our conscious mind to connect up and communicate with the various parts that make up the Interactive Mind Model, by using the Higher Self as an intermediary.

Through hypnosis, for example, we endeavour to communicate by linking up the conscious to the subconscious. When we undertake any physical therapy we are in a sense trying to connect our conscious to our physical self through touch and although this is a very basic and simple form of communication, it can nevertheless be extremely therapeutic.

There are several reasons why an individual would have difficulty connecting up to any of the parts of the Interactive Mind Model. There may be a communication blockage, which could have many and various causes, such as a lack of energy due to an emotional or physical blockage. Or there may be an incompatibility in the way one part 'talks' to the other. This would be similar to taking two computers, which use totally different programmes and software, and asking them to communicate with each other. Because of their incompatibility, one computer would be unable to recognise what the other was saying.

The function of the Em-Power Disc is to act as a Universal Translator allowing one system to communicate and interact with the other. Its primary function is to connect the conscious mind to the Higher Self, which in turn will communicate with any other system necessary in order to complete any task that we set for it. Its secondary function is to facilitate the connection between the conscious and

THE INTERACTIVE MIND MODEL

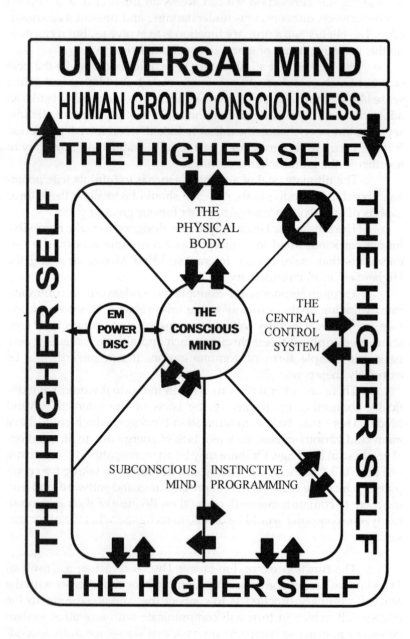

the subconscious without having to distract the conscious mind or place it in a hypnotic or relaxed state. *(See diagram "The Universal Translator", page 78).*

## HOW CAN WE TALK TO THE HIGHER SELF?

The Em-Power Healing System in conjunction with the Em-Power Disc enables your conscious mind to communicate with your Higher Self. Using a special system and carefully worded instructions we can establish this connection quite easily. In Em-Power Therapy we use the physical body to convey messages from the Higher Self. We simply ask the Higher Self to give a physical body movement that represents the word 'yes'. It could be anything from one or both arms lifting up to a rocking backwards or forwards. After establishing this 'yes' signal, we do the same for 'no' and will receive a completely different physical movement (physical signal). After we have established our 'yes' and 'no' physical signals it is possible to ask our Higher Self almost any question that requires a yes or no answer. Physical signals can be established for any word we choose, such as love, truth, good, bad, positive, negative, etc. In this way we can develop our own new and unique method of communicating through body language.

In hypnotherapy we try to make a connection with the subconscious mind by relaxing and distracting the conscious mind through hypnosis. Using this process it is also possible to receive physical 'yes' or 'no' signals that represent a communication coming from the subconscious mind. This is called an 'ideomotor response'. The problem with communicating with the subconscious mind as opposed to the Higher Self is that as we have said, the subconscious mind is like a six-year-old child and cannot distinguish between real or imaginary events. The subconscious is full of our fears and anxieties.

Another advantage of communicating through the Higher Self as opposed to talking directly to the subconscious mind (as in hypnosis) is that the Higher Self can act as a buffer and selection mechanism for information stored in the subconscious. The Higher Self can analyse all the information, which is recorded as if it were on video or audio tape, filtering out anything that is not relevant. It can tell the difference between a 'real' experience and something we have read, imagined or perhaps seen on TV or at the movies, whereas the subconscious on its own cannot. Indeed, hypnotherapists are now discovering that the Higher Self connection is more powerful than simply communicating with the subconscious mind.

*THE UNIVERSAL TRANSLATOR*

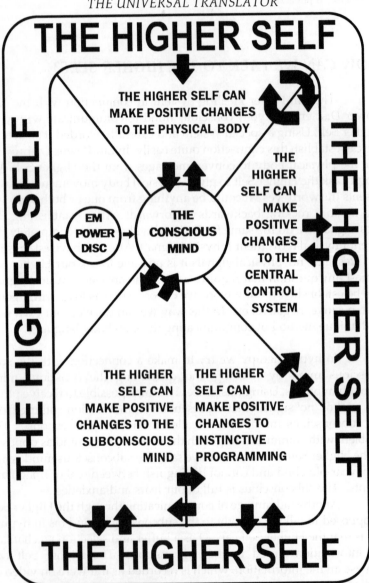

# HOW TO COMMUNICATE WITH THE HIGHER SELF AND MAKE POSITIVE CHANGES

When we want to make any changes in our perception (i.e. the way we feel or felt about a situation or event in the past), we can ask the Higher Self to scan our memory and change or adjust any of the unwanted negative emotional components. This can be done in various ways. For example, perhaps you would like to remove a specific phobia, which was caused by one event in your past. You could ask your Higher Self to change the negative component of that event, resulting in the removal of the phobia. Or you could ask the Higher Self to scan your entire memory, to go into each aspect and select any unnecessary negative emotional components, such as triggers that cause anger. In this particular instance the Higher Self would find each trigger - it could be anything from a person to an object - and change the negative emotional aspect of it. This can be tremendously powerful and uplifting. In a sense, we are removing old and unnecessary 'baggage' that we have been carrying around with us for years.

While the Higher Self is making changes on a physical level, many people experience movements of energy through and around the body. Then once the Higher Self has made changes in any system it will test the success of the process. For example, perhaps we have had a phobia of snakes and asked the Higher Self to work this through. It may then decide to create a dream involving snakes to test our emotional response and to make sure that we no longer feel distressed.

The Higher Self will only act in our best interests, for our highest good. It will only involve itself with the healing process if we give it specific instruction to do so. It is happy to watch and observe us in our everyday lives, taking a back seat so to speak. It will only interfere with our conscious and subconscious thought processes if we ask it to or if we accidentally put ourselves in a life-threatening situation.

There are certain instances in day-to-day life when we can become careless. Such as driving or getting out of a car. It is easy to be clumsy or preoccupied, not to look where you're going or to forget to check your mirror. Suddenly, something will stop you from opening the car door, or pulling out into the outside lane, or stepping out into the street. Had you done so, you wouldn't have seen the other car coming until it was too late. In situations like this, the Higher Self acting as a parent or guardian will often step in to save your life.

Like any good parent the Higher Self, if asked, can advise us on a course of action. If we take absolutely no notice, then it will not impose itself. On the contrary, it will allow us to make our own mistakes and learn in our own way. However, over a period of time, most people who regularly communicate with their Higher Self come to trust their connection and sooner or later take on board its advice and guidance. The Higher Self has limitless patience and understanding, always showing great compassion and love. Many people feel that true love is either 'missing' or has eluded them throughout their life. The love that the Higher Self gives can completely fill this void.

# THE LAWS OF HIGHER SELF COMMUNICATION

To communicate with the Higher Self and make changes to any other system within the Interactive Mind Model, certain rules apply. If we want to make positive changes on any level, we must first learn to talk to our Higher Self in the right way.

To trigger a desired response within the body or mind, we have to give an instruction to our Higher Self in the form of an affirmation. In Em-Power Therapy we call these affirmations 'command sequences'. Each command sequence must contain the following three components: purpose, direction and time scale. If any one of the three components is missing from a command sequence we give, our Higher Self will not be able to respond properly.

As these three elements are the basis for the entire communication process in Em-Power Therapy, it is important to clarify precisely what we mean by purpose, direction and time scale. *(See diagram 'Laws of Communication', page 82).*

### THE PURPOSE EQUATION = to evolve awareness in time.

The purpose is the result or effect that is intended or desired. For example, we may wish our Higher Self to correct a physical problem, such as a frozen shoulder. The purpose aspect in this example is 'to correct'. The purpose could be any of the following: *to correct, rebalance, normalise, optimise, increase, remove a negative, make a connection with, accept, retrieve, analyse information, etc.*

### THE DIRECTION EQUATION = the location of the desired action.

The direction is the mental or physical location where a specific response is desired. Examples are: *your shoulder, your knee, arm, subconscious, etc.*

### THE TIME SCALE EQUATION = a point(s) of action in time.

Time scale is the time frame in which you would like a specific action to take place. Time frames might be *'as soon as possible'*,

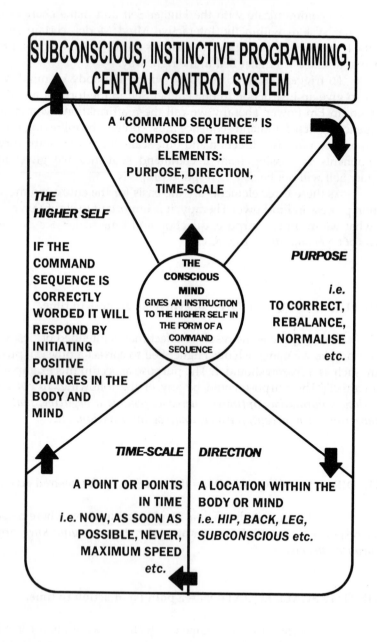

**SUBCONSCIOUS, INSTINCTIVE PROGRAMMING, CENTRAL CONTROL SYSTEM**

A "COMMAND SEQUENCE" IS COMPOSED OF THREE ELEMENTS: PURPOSE, DIRECTION, TIME-SCALE

*THE HIGHER SELF*

IF THE COMMAND SEQUENCE IS CORRECTLY WORDED IT WILL RESPOND BY INITIATING POSITIVE CHANGES IN THE BODY AND MIND

**THE CONSCIOUS MIND** GIVES AN INSTRUCTION TO THE HIGHER SELF IN THE FORM OF A COMMAND SEQUENCE

*PURPOSE*

i.e. TO CORRECT, REBALANCE, NORMALISE etc.

*TIME-SCALE*

A POINT OR POINTS IN TIME i.e. NOW, AS SOON AS POSSIBLE, NEVER, MAXIMUM SPEED etc.

*DIRECTION*

A LOCATION WITHIN THE BODY OR MIND i.e. HIP, BACK, LEG, SUBCONSCIOUS etc.

'now', a specific point in the future, a constant point like 'all the time', or even negative time such as 'never', (e.g. "I never want to experience such intense pain again"). When you start to use the Em-Power Healing System you will begin to understand why it is so important that the correct terminology is used when communicating with the Higher Self.

Many people who use the Em-Power Disc for the first time have commented that they feel compelled to say 'thank you' to show their gratitude, after every command sequence they give. Unfortunately saying 'thank you' is considered by the Higher Self as an acknowledgement that a task has been completed, and it will actually in many cases deactivate the command sequence that has just been made. This example illustrates that Em-Power Therapy works in a very precise way.

I have observed that some people have a misperception about the function of the Higher Self. They think that the Higher Self is actually an aspect of the subconscious mind and that if they believe or intend for something to happen then it will, regardless of what they say. In other words they believe that merely having intent is enough to make the changes they want. However, only the subconscious mind will respond to intent in this way.

Our Higher Self will not respond to intent alone but needs to be given precisely worded instructions using the purpose, direction and time-scale formula. It is only by using this formula that we can communicate with the Higher Self properly using the Disc. If you were to try to make a connection to communicate and interact with your Higher Self, then you would have to spend many years learning various advanced spiritual and meditative techniques. However, this connection is practically instantaneous when using the Em-Power Disc.

# THE POWER OF WORDS
# TO CHANGE YOUR LIFE

If I ask you to think about the word 'paradise', what immediately springs to mind? For one person it may be a tropical island with palm trees, gentle winds and the time to relax and feel the power of nature. For another it may be as simple as sitting by the fire on a cold winter's day with a good book and a cup of tea, or perhaps it could be simply having enough food to survive until tomorrow. For each of us the word 'paradise' triggers our imagination and a combination of both visual and emotional expectations and these are totally unique according to your past experiences. Depending on the word and who says it, a word can move a mountain or destroy a civilisation.

The Higher Self can access your subconscious mind and instinctive programming and provide you with feelings, emotions and physical responses that you can relate to and assimilate easily. For example, you could ask to feel 'wonderful', providing a command sequence is given in the correct way by using the equation, **purpose - direction - time scale,** *(i.e. "Make me feel wonderful now").* Your Higher Self will take this command, assess your subconscious memories, and find a point within your experience that constitutes a 'wonderful' feeling. Your Higher Self will then access the memory associated with that feeling and bring it forward into the conscious mind and physical body, so that you can experience it through the senses.

If you ask for a feeling or emotion that you have not experienced before, your Higher Self will have no other choice but to try and access your instinctive programming in an attempt to find the feeling. Your Higher Self may have to resort to accessing feelings on a primordial level. Tapping into this process in a controlled way using Em-Power Therapy is very positive and powerful. However, as with everything, to realise the potential benefits one has to experience it personally.

# HEALING THE FUTURE

All things within our existence appear to be constructed in some type of chain or flow pattern. If you drop a stone into a container full of still water, the ripples spread out, eventually reaching the edge. The action and power of the stone hitting the water causes a chain reaction that ripples through space and time. In fact, if you think about it, if you were to call the point at which the stone hits the water 'now', then all ripples that occur are in the 'future'. As far as we are concerned, everything we do, say and feel will ripple through time and space into our futures. Everything we see, hear, experience and store in our subconscious affects how we deal with each event and situation that happens after that point. This seems to be a rule of nature, a rule of time.

We can use this phenomenon to our advantage, taking in positive situations and information 'now', which will ripple and have positive effects in the future. Alternatively, were we to take in negative information, bad situations and events (real or imagined) they would ripple into the future creating problems.

As 'now' is already in the past, we cannot change it; but what happens next is up to you. It is really quite simple: put yourself into a relaxed mood by reading a book by the fire, or using the Em-Power Disc, or doing some exercise or listening to music. Make that image and understanding very clear in your mind and then send it into the future. No matter how silly this may sound, it will cause a ripple effect in time that will perpetuate your ability to relax, and make it stronger and more powerful with every second of each day. The more clearly we can define exactly what it is we want, then the more easily our Higher Self can create situations and events that will lead us towards achieving our goals.

I decided long ago that as I am experiencing 'now', the result of my past deeds, I would change my way of thinking so that the fruits of healing the future will come to me at some point. Literally, whatever you sow, you shall reap. Sow the good seeds, the positive feelings, good health and happiness and reap the rewards in the future. If good health is what you want then start now and change. Change what you eat, change the type of information you experience - read good books, watch insightful and positive TV or movies and stop perpetuating negative thoughts, fears and anxieties. Refrain from taking in information that has any kind of negative effect on your body, mind and spirit and you can create a new future for yourself based on your personal idea of paradise.

*THE THOUGHT PROCESS*

# THE HIGHER SELF

**THE "NOW" SITUATION STIMULATES OUR IMAGINATION WHICH TRIGGERS MEMORY WITHIN OUR SUBCONSCIOUS MIND**

**THE CONSCIOUS MIND TRIES TO APPLY LOGIC TO THE EMOTIONAL INFORMATION IT RECEIVES IN ORDER TO FORM A CONCLUSION**

**THE "NOW" SITUATION TRIGGERS THE THOUGHT PROCESS**

**THE SUBCONSCIOUS MIND IS STIMULATED BY OUR IMAGINATION WHICH CAN TRIGGER ASPECTS OF:
*INNER CHILD*
*CONDITIONING*
*MEMORIES AND EXPERIENCES***

**THE CONSCIOUS MIND RECEIVES EMOTIONALLY CHARGED INFORMATION FROM OUR INSTINCTIVE PROGRAMMING AND THE SUBCONSCIOUS MIND**

**OUR IMAGINATION ALSO STIMULATES OUR INSTINCTIVE PROGRAMMING TRIGGERING EMOTIONAL URGES, *e.g.*
*INHERITED*
*SURVIVAL*
*SPIRITUAL***

# THE HIGHER SELF

**THE HIGHER SELF OBSERVES AND WILL NOT INTERFERE UNLESS WE ARE IN A LIFE THREATENING SITUATION OR UNLESS WE ASK IT TO**

# THE THOUGHT PROCESS

Established psychology considers the thought process to be something that goes on purely in the subconscious and conscious mind. Em-Power Therapy, with its Interactive Mind Model, expands on this theory and takes into account other aspects of the self, such as our instinctive programming, central control system and the Higher Self. The diagram *("The Thought Process", on page 86)* illustrates our present understanding of the thought process using the Interactive Mind Model.

Every situation acts as a trigger for a thought process. With every thought, we use our imagination, which stimulates some of the components within the Interactive Mind Model (i.e. conscious mind, subconscious mind, instinctive programming, central control system and Higher Self). Our memories and experiences influence the way in which we respond to any particular situation and these experiences are stored in the subconscious mind. Therefore, aspects of the subconscious (such as the inner child cycle) and our conditioning can have an influence over any thought process. The inner child looks at the benefits and possibilities of any situation and draws an emotional conclusion. Similarly, our conditioning (the way our environment and upbringing shapes and moulds us) also greatly influences our thought process and generates a series of emotional conclusions. Hence the sum of the emotional conclusions of the subconscious mind form part of every thought process.

The same rules apply with our instinctive programming. All our inherited attributes have an influence over our thoughts and again the conclusions are emotional, but can trigger a physical response. For example, let's say someone asked you if you were hungry. The question itself stimulates the imagination, triggering responses from your instinctive programming and you may respond physically as well as emotionally. Your mouth may water slightly, or your tummy may feel hunger pangs as your memory provides ample information to remind you of your favourite foods.

The Higher Self observes each thought process but will not try to influence or interfere with it unless the process itself causes a life-threatening situation, or unless we actually ask it to intervene. It is possible, with the Em-Power Disc, to ask the Higher Self to both intervene and influence the thought process to help to clarify and realistically interpret any given situation.

In certain circumstances, experiences contained within the subconscious and information in the instinctive programming may trigger inappropriate emotional responses. Inappropriate responses are not beneficial to the individual and in such instances the Higher Self has the ability to make readjustments to help the person on a day-to-day basis.

If the Higher Self were included in the thought process on an ongoing basis, then it would act as a 'filtering' mechanism for the information contained within the subconscious mind and instinctive programming. This would allow us to respond to situations faster and in a more appropriate and balanced way. Our consciousness would in fact 'grow', as it would no longer be limited by our fears or negative imagination.

So what happens in a normal thought process is that all the various responses (from our subconscious and instinctive programming) are collected. The conscious mind tries to apply logic, drawing comparisons by using the information contained within the memory. Interestingly, when we try to draw a conclusion, the conscious mind will often attempt to use logic to explain away and justify illogical and sometimes irrational or emotional feelings.

Let us now consider a typical disagreement within any close relationship (with a partner or a parent for instance).Firstly, we have the idea of differing points of view - your point of view is based on your personal assessment and the same applies to your loved one. Regardless of who is right and who is wrong, if the disagreement turns into an argument our normal thought processes often become impaired due to the increased amount of emotion. Such emotions can easily cloud and distort our conclusions. Therefore if we ask the Higher Self to intervene we can avoid any misperceptions and improve our relationships.

However incredible it may sound, the thought process is one of energy conversion, from thought into action. Every situation is the stimulus and trigger for the motion of the energy flow. Thoughts stimulate and generate energy within our body and mind so we can survive and live. It is very true to say that as long as this thought process exists, then the possibilities for the recovery of damaged areas within the body and mind also exist. Our emotion gives direction to this energy and, depending on the emotion itself, the energy can subtly or drastically change.

Imagine a kitchen sink with hot and cold running water. Think of the cold water in this instance as negative energy and the hot as positive energy. Depending on the proportions of cold and hot water, the resulting temperature of the water collected in the sink could be anything from cold to warm. The more hot water is put into the cold, the more positive it is and the more cold water is put into the hot the more negative. But if we place equally proportionate amounts of hot and cold water into the sink at the same time, the temperature of the water in the sink will remain constant. If, however, we half fill the sink with cold water first and then add an equal amount of hot water to it, the resulting lukewarm water will have reached a certain temperature. But if we were to reverse this experiment and half fill the sink with hot water first, then add an equal amount of cold water to it, the resulting temperature (although we're using the same quantities as before), will be marginally lower because the hot water has had time to cool down a couple of degrees.

The same thing happens to our thoughts. If we have a negative thought first and then a positive thought immediately afterwards, the resulting energy will be more positive. If we have a positive thought first and then a negative one afterwards, it takes the power away and reduces the overall positive aspect of the energy.

How many times have you heard the question "Which do you want first, the good news or the bad news?" Most people, confronted with this question opt for the bad news first. This may not be a conscious effort to try to neutralise the negative aspects of the information that they are about to receive. It may simply be a subconscious or instinctive 'knowing' that if we place a positive after a negative, it will have the effect of reducing or neutralising the negative.

The thought processes that we have on a second-by-second basis provide energy to the body and mind. The more negative the thought process is, the less energy is available overall. Consequently, it is more difficult for a pessimistic person, or one who thinks negatively, to recover from injury or illness on a physical or emotional level. So if we increase the amount of positive thought we can improve and increase the energy flow around the body and mind.

Generally speaking, the more positive the thoughts are on an ongoing basis, the more energy is being made available to us. Since thinking positively all the time is impossible for most people, ideally we need a management system that will automatically provide a positive thought after every negative one we have. The idea being to neutralise the effects of the negative energy and to improve the energy flow around the body and mind.

If we have equal amounts of negative and positive thoughts then eventually our reserves of energy within our being will diminish. The ability of the immune system to fight off diseases will improve, and the recovery time of an injury will be reduced while the ability of the Em-Power Disc to help a person make positive changes will increase. So we need a simple mental process that we can use to quickly neutralise negative thoughts, by introducing more powerful positive thoughts. 'The Thought Management System' will do this.

Spiritual energy, however, cannot be negative and can be used to increase and reinforce the energy created by positive emotions. We can stimulate and raise the level of spiritual energy in a very simple way, by increasing our diet of positive spiritual concepts through discussion and ideas. Whether or not we believe in the concept of God, by simply discussing it we build up and enhance our awareness of our spiritual side, thus creating more spiritual energy and improving our Higher Self connection.

# THE THOUGHT MANAGEMENT SYSTEM

The first thing that we need to do is to use the Em-Power Disc and our connection to our Higher Self to create a management system. This is intended to regulate the quantity of negative thoughts we have and will be used to develop an energy conversion system that will spontaneously change negative thoughts and energy into positive. This will provide the body and mind with all the energy it needs to operate successfully and with the ability to make any necessary changes when we ask it to.

The fundamental basis for a management system must take into account the rules that apply within the subconscious mind, central control system, instinctive programming and Higher Self. Most importantly 'like attracts like' and similar thoughts will attract each other. Positive thought processes will attract more positive thoughts and vice versa.

## TRIGGERS FOR POSITIVE IMAGERY

Some people may view their life as being totally negative in every way and believe there is nothing positive for them. Nevertheless, however sweeping and ridiculous the following statement may seem, you will find that it is true: "There is a positive component within every situation". This statement may cause a major conflict within some belief systems. As a reader, you may see images of torture and starvation and then ask the question, "So where's the positive component in that?"

If we take an extreme example of a negative, such as starvation, hunger and despair in the third world, we can find a positive, for example being aware of such injustices can actually make us more appreciative of what 'we' have.

There are many examples where athletes with one leg can run faster than a healthy person with two! The good or positive is in the appreciation and admiration here. The difficulty is when we are not aware that there is a problem in the first place. It is impossible to completely cure an alcoholic of his addiction, for example, if he doesn't perceive that he actually has a drink problem.

There are unknown situations in life, (and death is one of them), that can create fear and anxiety because we can allow our negative imagination to create something that doesn't exist. The key to removing all fear is truth: *"The truth will set you free"*. The only way to seek out the truth is to ask the Higher Self to allow us to become aware of it. It is really important that we do not communicate with the subconscious mind here, as it is limited to the information and fears contained within our memory. If we have trouble in recalling or creating a positive image, then we can ask the Higher Self to find one for us and it will do this, providing we prevent the subconscious mind from interfering.

# CREATING THE THOUGHT MANAGEMENT SYSTEM

*(See diagram "The Thought Management System", page 94)*

Firstly, we need to build up an arsenal of positive thoughts and images from any point in our lives. These positive thoughts do not necessarily have to be considered to be 'happy' ones. For example, I asked a patient of mine to give me the best example of her positive thought. I could tell that this was quite hard for her and nothing sprang to mind easily. After a few moments she told me of an experience. She had been in a large toy store Christmas shopping when several severely disabled children and adolescents were wheeled in with their carers. One particular guy attracted her attention.

"I'd been feeling a bit down that day," she said. "It was nothing major, nothing I could put my finger on even. Just the pressure of my work and trying to find time to do my shopping. I was just about to join the queue when I noticed this boy in a wheelchair. He was very severely disabled, he only had arms and a head and no body to speak of. Seeing him came as a major shock to me, I couldn't work out where his body was, where his organs were. I was conscious at that moment that I might be staring and I didn't want to appear rude and so I looked away. Then I immediately felt embarrassed about looking away. He joined the queue in front of me.

"Because of his shape, lots of people were looking at him now, but trying not to look if you know what I mean. The amazing thing about this guy was that he was so totally unfazed by this. You could tell, just by his very attitude that despite his disability and people's reactions to it, he was getting on with his life, doing his own thing. He was just so together. I started to feel sorry for him, imagining what it must be like, then I thought, 'Why am I doing this?' It's so patronising. He didn't seem to appear to be feeling sorry for himself and he didn't seem to be the type of guy who would have appreciated such emotions from others or me. I felt this overwhelming sense of complete admiration and respect for him. He made me feel pathetic and I'm not embarrassed to say it, he did make me feel lucky and he gave me perspective. I was in awe of him."

Our positive thoughts and experiences are not always the most obvious ones. They could be anything from a sunset to the birth of your baby; a graduation or childhood achievement to a simple observation. It's whatever is personal and means something to you, but pick the most powerful image for you. When you have thought of it, close your eyes and go back in time to approximately five minutes before this special event.

*THE THOUGHT MANAGEMENT SYSTEM*

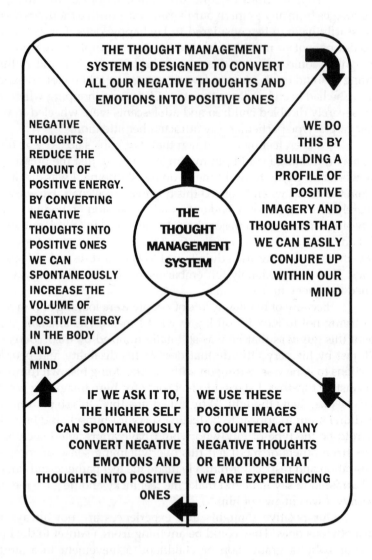

THE THOUGHT MANAGEMENT SYSTEM IS DESIGNED TO CONVERT ALL OUR NEGATIVE THOUGHTS AND EMOTIONS INTO POSITIVE ONES

NEGATIVE THOUGHTS REDUCE THE AMOUNT OF POSITIVE ENERGY. BY CONVERTING NEGATIVE THOUGHTS INTO POSITIVE ONES WE CAN SPONTANEOUSLY INCREASE THE VOLUME OF POSITIVE ENERGY IN THE BODY AND MIND

THE THOUGHT MANAGEMENT SYSTEM

WE DO THIS BY BUILDING A PROFILE OF POSITIVE IMAGERY AND THOUGHTS THAT WE CAN EASILY CONJURE UP WITHIN OUR MIND

IF WE ASK IT TO, THE HIGHER SELF CAN SPONTANEOUSLY CONVERT NEGATIVE EMOTIONS AND THOUGHTS INTO POSITIVE ONES

WE USE THESE POSITIVE IMAGES TO COUNTERACT ANY NEGATIVE THOUGHTS OR EMOTIONS THAT WE ARE EXPERIENCING

*"SPONTANEOUSLY CONVERTS NEGATIVE THOUGHTS AND ENERGY INTO POSITIVE ENERGY"*

In sequence re-live the experience, remember the various components: what you could see, how you felt, the smells and visual images, what was said. Travel a bit further with your imagination and look around you. This five-minute lead up is very important as it is your starting point and sets the scene. Then re-live your experience, moving through time until you are at the point approximately five minutes after your positive event and stop it there. Now take a pen and paper and answer the following:

1)     What could you see? Describe in as much detail as possible the things you visualised in your experience. Note the colours and textures. How vivid was it? Do this for all the five senses - sight, hearing, touch, smell and taste.

2)     Make a list of all the emotions you felt. Were you happy? Did you feel elated or excited? Joyful? Tender?

3)     Now examine each description and the main triggers of your experience. For example, you may have re-lived your tenth birthday and remember getting lots of presents, but one in particular was from your grandma. It was a book wrapped in gold crinkly paper, which felt silky to touch. You opened it just after you blew out the candles on your birthday cake and you could still smell the candle wax. Everyone was singing happy birthday to you. In this instance your triggering words may be **'love, grandma, happy birthday, candles, presents'**.

Follow this procedure for three or four really positive situations. If you can't find really positive ones, then build up a volume of say ten fairly positive ones instead. To test it out, pick a situation in your life that wasn't so good. Imagine this negative event in the same way as you did with the positive one, but at the end key in your positive words to counteract the negative situation and see how it makes you feel.

The above exercises can be achieved much faster and more easily by connecting to the Higher Self through the Em-Power Disc and asking it to activate a similar process. To do this, the Higher Self will scan the sum of our experiences contained in the subconscious mind, identifying and selecting what it considers to be the most positive situations. It will then take the positive essence from all these events, holding it as one huge overall positive trigger. Once the Higher Self has created and activated this new trigger, it will be so powerful that no negative situation or event can ever override it.

This is the basis of the Thought Management System. In addition there are various techniques built into this process to prevent subconscious interference. This is because often the subconscious mind believes that negative memories and fears serve a useful purpose of some kind. It may, in all honesty, consider these negative elements to be not only of benefit to you, but also necessary for your protection. In other words the subconscious needs to be convinced, and in a sense has to be taught by the Higher Self, about the reasons why it is no longer necessary for it hold these negative fears and feelings. It is only by doing this that the subconscious mind will 'freely' give up the negativity it has been harbouring and which we experience on a daily basis throughout our lives.

The next stage is to take the negative energy held in the subconscious mind and convert it into positive energy not only in the past but also in the present and future too. The same process must take place within the instinctive programming and we can do this by asking the Higher Self to remove any emotional components that could cause unnecessary misperceptions. But first we must ask the Higher Self to look at and examine the sum of the information contained within our instinctive programming, remove all unnecessary aspects therein, and re-examine the information to see if we need to add any positive or additional programming that would help not only ourselves but also future generations.

When we have given these commands to the Higher Self, we will then ask it to continuously stimulate the level of spiritual energy and plant a safety valve within our being to protect us from the negative aspects of our subconscious and instinctive programming. This whole process can be ongoing and will eventually become permanent.

## ACTIVATING
## THE ENERGY CONVERSION SYSTEM

At this moment in time we are not aware of any other method of activating spontaneous energy conversion within the mind and body that does not involve communication through the Higher Self.

Using Em-Power Therapy, the Higher Self can activate this energy conversion process effortlessly. Providing that we give a simple set of instructions or 'command sequences', the Higher Self can literally and spontaneously convert negative energy into positive.

# LIVING WITH THE MIND

When we are all brought into this world, each one of us is unique and special in our own way yet we are cut off from ourselves in a number of ways. Our education process, for instance, does not teach us the workings of the mind or give us rules to help us understand it. Although this is the most fundamental and basic part of our being, nobody fully understands how the mind truly works. We are literally expected to go through our lives like emotional 'sky-divers' who have not received any actual training before jumping out of the plane.

Let's develop this metaphor further. Just imagine that you had to put on a parachute and jump out of a plane without knowing what to do! You would have to learn how to control your parachute during your descent. As we are all different, we would all learn the skills of parachuting at different rates. Also, depending on the atmospheric and weather conditions, the descent could be anything from calm serenity, to a 'white-knuckled' roller coaster ride! Obviously it would be more difficult to learn to control a parachute in turbulent weather than it would be in steady conditions. Calm weather would give you more time to master your skill and help you understand the process of your descent.

But wouldn't it be much better if we could all learn how to control every aspect of our descent, regardless of the weather conditions, before we jumped out of the plane?

As we are all 'emotional sky-divers', it would be useful for us to be more aware of some common symptoms that we may feel during this descent:

*Shortness of breath*
*Variations in body temperature - such as sweating, feeling hot and sticky, particularly on the palms of the hands*
*Feeling dizzy*
*Irritable bowels/bladder*
*Panicking - the need to escape*
*Sharp pains in the extremities, such as hands and feet*
*Nausea*
*Headaches*
*Lack of co-ordination/stuttering*
*Insecurity*
*Fears/phobias - e.g. heights, enclosed spaces, spiders, flying, etc.*
*Fear of the unknown*
*Pessimism*
*Stress*
*A sense of vulnerability.*

Everyone, without exception, has these feelings and reactions on some level at some point in their lives. So however anxious, fearful or distressed you may feel you are, remember that there are literally millions of others who feel exactly the same way! All these symptoms are associated with:

**Depression**
**Anxiety**
**Fear**
**Worry**

We try to protect ourselves from feeling these symptoms by:

*Avoiding situations*
*Detachment*
*Disassociation with people and situations*
*Reclusiveness*
*Emotional self-imprisonment*
*Avoiding intimacy with others*
*Aggressiveness, in order to avoid a situation*
*Either shouting, or talking quietly*
*Avoiding any kind of change*
*Being very controlling of others in order to feel more secure*
*Extreme behaviour; finding ways of 'escape'*
*Taking alcohol or drugs to try to desensitise our emotions to avoid physical symptoms.*

To make any real positive changes in our lives we must develop improved control over ourselves. The only way this can be done is by acknowledging and accepting that these feelings exist in the first place. Then we can examine our own symptoms to help find ways to make it easier for us to properly and successfully deal with everyday situations on a lifelong basis. Many people have achieved this by undergoing various kinds of therapy. It is vital to understand the processes involved and move forward, thus avoiding the road of self-indulgence where we allow our negativity and fears to perpetuate.

A lot of people are not prepared to make changes in order to take charge of their lives. All they really want is for somebody or something else to remove the symptoms of their depression or anxieties, often through medication. However, the only way we can deal with this situation permanently is to develop improved control of our physical and emotional responses to given situations.

When I use the word 'control' I do not mean suppression of our emotions or physical responses. I mean the 're-management' of our emotions; to be able to form new and more positive thought processes, which will in turn enable us to remove negative physical feelings associated with depression and anxiety. In other words, not only must we remove the symptoms on a long-term basis; we must also develop easy and habitual management techniques that give us more control over our body and mind.

Using Em-Power Therapy, we can ask the Higher Self to help It will usually prove itself by removing the emotional and physical symptoms instantaneously, giving a person the breathing space required to become more rational and able to see things for what they really are. When using the Em-Power Disc, many people initially report that most of the symptoms of their anxiety - depression or fear - almost completely disappear within the first three to six weeks. We call this period the 'emotional buffer zone'. The Higher Self needs to prove to us that it can help and it does this by physically removing symptoms. After this initial period, the Higher Self will then try to help us to develop more control of our 'perception' of situations and our environment.

At this point, the Higher Self may re-activate some symptoms, but in a very controlled way, to help and enable us to improve our rational thinking. In other words, it will recreate the fear or anxiety in a precisely 'managed' way that will enable one to rationalise a situation and control it relatively easily. It's almost as if we are being given little tests to pass. These 'tests' are specifically designed to build up our confidence and management skills. Then, as situations become more complex, our increased confidence will reduce our anxiety. Hence, if a major or unavoidable situation were to suddenly occur, a person could handle it purely because they hadn't sheltered themselves. As a result, we would be able to deal with anything in life. *(See diagram "Living with the Mind", page 100).*

As in life and mathematics, the best way to achieve our goal is to split each problem into component parts and tackle each part a bit at a time. Then we will find that, as we understand more and more of the process, we will be able to handle more without even realising it.

Understanding the process that our Higher Self uses to achieve the best results for each and everyone of us removes the feeling of the 'unknown'. If we actually 'know' what is about to happen before it happens, it removes our fear of the unknown, and as we build up positive experiences by learning that we can face any situation that life may throw our way, each one of these changes is welcomed and not avoided.

*LIVING WITH THE MIND*

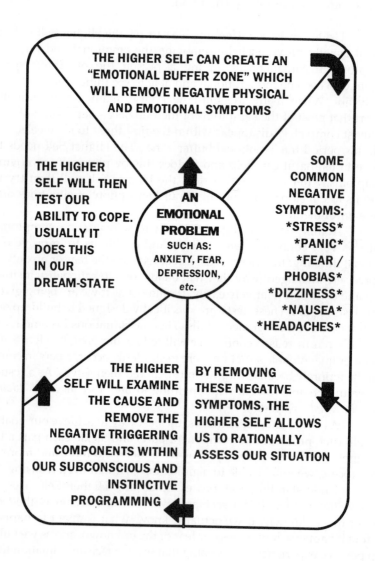

# THE DIFFERENCE BETWEEN EM-POWER THERAPY AND HYPNOSIS

We can use the rules of the subconscious mind to greatly alleviate symptoms. Hypnotherapy and psychotherapy use various techniques to try and persuade the subconscious mind to adjust our perceptions, so that we may more clearly interpret, understand and perceive our responses. Many people misperceive the therapeutic benefits of hypnosis because of stage hypnotists and performers, which have given rise to much bad press over recent years. There are many ways that hypnosis and other psychotherapeutic techniques can trick the mind positively, removing phobias and physical symptoms associated with fear. It is the same trickery that hypnotists use to persuade the mind into believing that you are eating an apple when you are in fact eating an onion. I personally find the quirks of the mind to be very interesting but believe that this kind of stage hypnosis, which is entertaining for many, is of no benefit to the people taking part.

It is a natural instinct of ours to try and find a reasonable explanation for how something works. 'Self hypnosis' and 'the power of the mind' are explanations that have been given for the workings of the Em-Power Disc. However, Em-Power Therapy is NOT self-hypnosis or simply 'the power of the mind'. Almost anything can fall within the context of 'the power of the mind' - from the invention of the television set, to yoga techniques. In fact there is nothing in existence that doesn't fall within the realms of 'the power of the mind'.

In hypnosis we use relaxation techniques to enter into a hypnotic state so that we can make suggestions to the subconscious mind. These suggestions take the form of 'affirmations' that are constructed in a very precise manner. The basic rules for such affirmations are:

*All affirmations must be given in the present tense e.g. *"I am feeling lighter and lighter..."*

*All affirmations have to be repeated many, many times to enable the subconscious mind to respond to them.

*As the subconscious mind thinks like a six-year-old child, all affirmations must be kept very simple.

*Not everyone can become relaxed enough to make a suggestion or affirmation work for them.

When we use Em-Power Therapy we are communicating with a different part of the mind and body, known as the Higher Self. This is a benevolent intelligence that we all possess. Its sole purpose is to serve and protect us, acting as our guide and conscience throughout our life.

The fundamental difference between communicating with the subconscious mind and talking with the Higher Self is that the Higher Self is a supreme intellect, capable of complex, interactive communication. The Higher Self will only respond to direct commands given in a very precise manner and it will not respond to suggestions, as they are not specific enough. The basic rules for Em-Power Therapy and communication with the Higher Self are:

*All commands must follow the equation, *purpose, direction and time scale.*

*Command sequences are not interpreted using imagination. All responses are based on the precise nature of the command.

*Most people are capable of communication with the Higher Self using the Em-Power Disc.

*It is not necessary for a person to be in a relaxed or hypnotic state.

So it may be easier to explain away the phenomenon of the Em-Power Disc by trying to associate it with other therapies, but in actual fact it is totally unique and independent. The Em-Power Disc exists on its own terms, and for best results one must work within its perimeters, keeping an open mind at all times.

# THE EGO TRAP

The 'ego' is a ball and chain that shackles our development throughout our entire life. Many people use the word 'pride' to describe something that is in actual fact ego. Having pride in one's work and achievements should mean an inner satisfaction that we have literally done our best whatever that may be, whether we are a mathematician trying to unravel the equation of the universe or a person who takes 'pride' in the growth of the flowers he has planted.

Ego is different. It is a spectre, which preys upon the soul of our very existence, restricting personal growth and development. All people, perhaps with the exception of saints, fall into the ego trap.

When communicating with the Higher Self and the body, we must try to remove as much of the ego as possible. Where another person is using psychological and therapeutic techniques with a patient, it is relatively easy for the ego of an individual to interfere with the healing process. Fortunately, when using the Em-Power Disc and Em-Power Therapy, we almost instantly connect with our Higher Self, which is void of any ego. This enables almost any individual to by-pass this negative aspect of each and every one of us.

Often, after the initial experience of using the Em-Power Disc, a conflict between the ego and the Higher Self can occur. This conflict is very short-lived for most people who truly wish to become more fulfilled. On the one hand, the ego will say "I am better than most and perhaps not in need of assistance from my Higher Self". Knowing this to be the case, the Higher Self usually tries to prove its worth to us on levels that can by-pass the ego. It might do this by correcting a physical problem or endowing us with a new and incredible ability. Usually as a person develops, they begin to comprehend that the more they know, the more they realise they don't know! This understanding ultimately unshackles a person from the ego, allowing them to develop in their own unique and special way.

In the case of Em-Power Therapy, we must learn to trust in the Higher Self through practical, positive experiences. Developing this trust will absolutely guarantee that you will transcend your present day thinking and evolve yourself on all levels - mental, spiritual and emotional.

I receive many calls from people who find it difficult to come to terms with the fact that their Higher Self is able to make such profound physical and emotional changes, seemingly beyond their conscious control. They often admit that it is their ego which prevents them from comfortably relinquishing control to their Higher Self.

Many view the Higher Self as some kind of 'alien or external force', although after reasoning with their fears logically, they do come to realise that in fact this isn't the case and that the Higher Self is only a benevolent extension of themselves. The problem can exist because a person has put limitations on their own abilities, and when they surpass these limitations - often in leaps and bounds - they become a little insecure. They start to believe that it wasn't really them at all, but that some outside force or influence has interfered with them in some way.

I recall the first time I visited a planetarium. The awe and amazement of the universe struck an immediate chord within my very soul.I realised that I was merely a 'speck of dust' upon a planet, which itself was only a 'speck of dust' within the solar system, which in turn is a 'speck' in the universe. This feeling of being so small instantly reduced the level of my ego by ninety-nine percent! I am sure it would have achieved one hundred percent if I could have truly got my mind around the enormous and unlimited scale of the universe. Later, I realised that it was my arrogance that allowed me to think that both the human race and I were in any way superior in accomplishments or intelligence. In fact, given the scale of possibilities of life existing in other worlds and dimensions, we were perhaps even less than a speck upon a speck!

The effects of the signal from the Em-Power Disc allow most people to immediately activate simple 'yes' or 'no' signals, or a spontaneous exercise. A 'yes' or 'no' signal is a physical body movement which represents a 'yes' or 'no' communication coming directly from the Higher Self.

For example, we could ask a simple question like "Are oranges good for me?" and we would receive in response a physical movement representing either 'yes' or 'no'. With the Em-Power Healing System, we can receive physical body signals from the Higher Self for literally anything that exists within the external world, and also describe anything that exits within our conscious and subconscious mind. A large part of the therapy itself involves information about our lives and decision-making processes. This information is expressed and communicated to us through the physical body so the movements are a kind of body language.

Many people have contacted me, excited about the fact that they have been 'honoured' by the universe because they can trigger these simple physical responses. Then some say that they no longer need the Em-Power Disc, as they have learned to do it for themselves. This reaction seems to me rather like a young child saying to his mother, "Mom, I can look after myself now because I can make peanut butter sandwiches, tuck myself into bed and take milk from the fridge". As a parent would you allow that child out onto the street to make his or her own way in life? I doubt it! But as we are all adults we have to make decisions for ourselves.

If a medical student, for example, wants to become a surgeon, most would agree that learning to become a surgeon would take more than one simple lesson. If the medical student turned to the teacher after the first lesson and said "I now know everything. Let me operate on the next patient", the teacher would naturally be annoyed at the student and perhaps even refuse to continue to teach him or her. The way of the world is that one must experience in order to learn properly and, in many instances, study is no replacement for practical experience. It is only the ego of the student that prevents them from achieving their goals. In other words, if you already know everything, then what else is there to learn? The geniuses on the planet realise that the more they learn, the more there is to learn. I don't think that one actually needs to be a genius to figure this out, but any teacher would have more time for the student who is prepared to learn than for the student who thinks they know everything.

On a personal note, in my past I have been a victim of 'ego', allowing my own feelings of misguided superiority to restrict my personal and spiritual growth. I can look back now upon my life with an internal grin, because I realise that the times when I felt most superior and allowed my ego to rule were in fact empty and wasted. So, if any of you ask "What can the Em-Power Disc do for me?", my reply would have to be - anything, within the limits of your imagination! The possibilities of what you can actually achieve are so limitless, yet many people will still ask me, "What can I use the Disc for?" They cannot get their minds around the unlimited possibilities and potential that exists within their connection to their Higher Self. Literally anything is possible, providing that you know how to ask the right questions.

# SPIRITUAL ENLIGHTENMENT

The quest for spiritual enlightenment has been the sole purpose of many people for thousands of years. Many over the centuries have asked the question "Am I more than a physical body?". Often an extraordinary event triggers this unquenchable passion to uncover who and what we are. Philosophers ponder the infinite possibilities of the afterlife, those new dimensions where our everlasting souls dwell in wondrous worlds. Our limited perceptions determine the possibilities and likelihood of a spiritual realm of existence. I personally believe in the concept of a spiritual realm that exists somewhere on another plane or dimension, where our physical bodies cannot exist: a place of pure energy and thought.

Can dreaming about a spiritual realm make it exist? Perhaps it can, as most of our reality begins with a thought, an idea, or dream. If we were incapable of dreaming and making our dreams a reality we would be the same as the other animals on the earth, who are totally dependent on their environment. However, the human race has transcended its primitive animal instincts and has used its imagination (negative and positive) to mould the world into a manifestation of our innermost desires and fears. This has often happened at the expense of our environment. Indeed we are on the verge between self-destruction and spiritual development with the scales tipping towards self-destruction. Yet perhaps we should consider that by destroying our eco-system on Earth, we may in turn be causing an impact on an interplanetary level or even on an interdimensional level. We don't really know, but our ignorance is no excuse, as our actions may well be having an impact on the well being of others in our world or who may exist on other planes.

The gurus of our world preach a message of inner wisdom, which states that all knowledge of all things exists within each and everyone of us. I do not consider myself to be a guru but I certainly agree with this message. The question is how do we uncover this inner wisdom to help ourselves and our world? The knowledge or information we receive from this inner wisdom is only as good as the questions we ask. Indeed the fundamental aim of this book is to help you find the way to ask the right questions for yourself.

Some people who consider themselves to be 'spiritually aware' show a kind of elitist attitude. These people may have read many books on the subject and perhaps even visited gurus in such places as India and Tibet on their quest for enlightenment. Unfortunately along the way some have become side-tracked by technicalities, concepts and principles and the rules set by so-called 'spiritually enlightened' individuals. This dogma has only served to cloud the truth, and in fact often results in self-imprisonment of our spirituality within the boundaries and limitations of our imagination and subconscious experiences.

In life, it is always the experience itself that counts and not the description of it. Anything that does not trigger a personal experience is mere commentary. Often spiritual matters have been kept secret and in many cases we are only fed certain bits of information. This is a 'mystery-mastery' technique, whereby control is kept by keeping the 'student' in constant suspense and anticipation.

So what is spirituality? To me, it means being one with the 'source' of our existence. Viewing life with the eyes of hope and freedom - the freedom to choose the 'good' in something, to emphasise the positive and find ways to remove or avoid the negative.

As previously stated, the principles in this book do not require faith in the conventional religious sense of the word. Your goal may be to become more 'spiritual', but you need to establish what that really means. What do you feel spirituality means for you? We need to clearly define this on a personal level so that we can plot an appropriate course of action in order to reach our desired, personal destination.

Spirituality means different things for different people. What one person may call 'a search for spirituality' another may consider merely 'self-development'. For me, trusting in one's own inner strength and wisdom and searching within that wisdom is the true path of spirituality. I personally believe that those who search in places other than within themselves are on a detour of self-denial.

Often it is true that searching externally for something can stimulate an internal recognition or trigger and give a set of co-ordinates and a direction. This trigger can come from literally anywhere: from the traditional method of going on a journey to perhaps some holy or religiously significant place, or from merely looking at a beautiful flower in a field of thorns.

Imagine a book that contains the answer to any question you could conceivably ask - and that this book is written as a kind of computer programme inside you. You may be aware that this book exists, but for some unknown reason you cannot find it and think that you might have lost it. So, you decide to focus your attention and look for this book in the external world by going on various spiritual quests. But you never seem to be able to find it. This is because if we do not know and recognise the book when it is in our own possession, we certainly would not recognise it if we were searching amongst thousands of other books.

What I am trying to say here is that it is not necessary to live a life of denial or to go on endless spiritual journeys, unless that is something you particularly like doing. In fact, you never even have to leave the confines of your own mind and imagination. This is not some kind of special secret, although there are methods by which you can redirect your focus inwardly and increase your connection with your spiritual side such as meditation, yoga and Tai Chi. However, there is a simpler way for most. Find the special book or programme inside you, and look up the answer to your spiritual question.

Spirituality is an awareness and understanding of the laws of nature and other dimensions. You can question your Higher Self by using the Em-Power Disc on a simple level. But the first step is to heighten and enhance your awareness of the spiritual realms and dimensions.

Here is just one technique that you may wish to try with or without an Em-Power Disc. You can use any object in nature. I personally recommend finding a secluded spot either in a wooded area or by the beach. If you are in a built-up city, find the quietest place in your home and take with you a really beautiful flower or something else from nature that you can focus on. The object of this exercise is to expand your awareness by trying to become 'one' with the flower, tree or sea, etc. This process is easy for some and more difficult for others. You could imagine your flower, tree or waves as living, breathing natural forces of nature. For instance, as the waves break on the shoreline, imagine that the sea is breathing in and out. Or that, as its branches move gently in the breeze, the tree is breathing the carbon dioxide in and releasing the oxygen out. The idea is to try and match your breathing with the sea, the tree or flower.

As you become more in-sync with nature, your awareness automatically begins to expand. All the senses are heightened, to the extent whereby you can almost hear each breath and see the life that exists within nature. Once you find this place within your mind it is like a new state of consciousness, and you can subtly move within it, stimulating new states of being. It isn't absolutely necessary, but it is usually helpful to stand during this process so that you can move gently with the motions of the element of nature in your focus.

Once you have made the connection within yourself you will become aware of the place in your mind and body where the feeling is coming from. I personally find the connection on a physical level to be stronger when I focus on my breathing. Imagine this place in your body, wherever it may be, as a kind of living ball of light, which expands and contracts as you breathe. Connected to this ball of light are threads or tentacles of thin but very strong light, like highways leading to new, exciting places. All you need to do is to try and find one of these roads in your mind and follow it to see where it leads. This entire process is a combination of visual and physical focusing that is almost identical to the meditative process.

Another method or visualisation you could try is to imagine a large bud or yellow flower that has not blossomed yet. Visualise each petal unfolding, with a bright light radiating from the centre. As the petals open, the light becomes brighter and your body becomes lighter. The light represents your personal connection to the source. When you see and can picture the image in your mind ask your Higher Self or consciousness to connect you to your concept of God. Visualise this Godliness growing as the petals of the flower open wider and wider, reaching the ultimate connection when you see the centre of your flower in your mind.

By using the Em-Power Disc, you can enhance your experience of this phenomenon and expand your consciousness in directions that you never dreamed possible. For some people the initial experience may be very powerful but as you get used to making and connecting with your Higher Self and your concept of God, you will become more accustomed to the sensations and the incredible power of the energy you are tapping into.

If you are a healer or wish to try spiritual healing on a friend or member of your family, try this in conjunction with the Em-Power Disc and your connection with your spiritual side will increase and improve considerably. This will allow you to channel your powers on a spiritual level (i.e. spiritual healing). It is much, much easier to connect using the Disc, rather than using visualisations.

# SPIRITUAL HEALING

Spiritual healing has been practised for thousands of years in one form or another all over the world. Many spiritual healers have had incredible and inexplicable successes in treating a multitude of problems including so-called 'incurable' and terminal conditions, such as cancer and organ failure. In spiritual healing, the healer allows him or herself to become a channel for a special kind of 'godly' energy.

I have tremendous respect for spiritual healers, although some of their organisations have over the years become bureaucratic. It is said that anyone is capable of spiritual healing. It does not require faith of any kind by the patient, but the healer is often a very spiritually aware person whose main goal in life is to help others. He or she often has a very strong belief in God as the inexplicable force that can cure any problem. This belief develops in the healer after years of experience, and although there are several young spiritual healers, the most powerful and successful ones such as Harry Edwards, John Cain, Matthew Manning and Betty Shine have been healing for many, many years. It would be difficult for anyone to ignore their amazing and incredible gifts as well as their successes.

Some spiritual healers also have clairvoyant abilities, which they use as part of their healing process on a more emotional level. Many healers of spiritual healing and Reiki as well as some of the less well-known forms of healing use the Em-Power Disc. The Disc enhances their connection with the energy that they are already channelling.

# 'GOD', THE ULTIMATE CONNECTION

The word 'God' has incredible healing powers irrespective of whether we personally believe in the concept. Because many people do believe in a 'God', the word itself attracts positive energy to those who evoke it. But who can explain God? It is such a personal thing that universal comprehension is impossible.

The body can do the most amazing things, including healing itself, thinking and housing our consciousness. But when we wish to go beyond our limited concepts and experiences, we turn to the one force that is void of any limitations.

The word 'faith' often comes hand in glove with many people's concept of 'God'. Often faith can be described as a blind trust. However, only the concept of 'God' is deserving of such faith. It is amazing and awe-inspiring that it is possible to believe in the concept of 'God' without having 'blind faith'. Experiences exist within each person's life that can prove without any doubt the existence of 'God'.

I personally believe in the concept of an ultimate force that guides our existence. Through the Higher Self it is possible for most of us to receive all the proof we need, so one's faith will grow through practical, physical and emotional experiences. It seems that all we really need to do is ask to experience the concept of 'God' through the Higher Self, because somehow 'God' always seems to reveal 'itself' in terms we can feel, experience, and share with others.

The Em-Power Disc connects you up with your Higher Self, which in turn can allow you to experience the concept of God. However, the Higher Self also has its limitations (just like the physical body does), so if you are asking for something that transcends the possibilities of the physical body and Higher Self, your questions should be directed to 'God'.

# HOW TO FIND YOUR PURPOSE IN LIFE

We are all links within the chain of life, all intricate parts of a web that supports other lives in the chain and we are all equally important. Even the greatest leaders in the world would never have existed without the presence of specific individuals.

The best example of this is the influence our parents have over our lives, in the most basic positive and negative ways. You may be the great-grandmother of some future person that solves the fundamental problems of the world. However insignificant any one person may feel him or herself to be, their perception and feelings are purely personal and totally emotionally-driven. We make a difference to those around us, whether that difference is good or bad. So, the question that should be asked here is not "What is my purpose?" but rather "What is my *best* purpose?".

When we ask ourselves this question, as we all do from time to time, most people directly communicate with their Higher Self. But what is the intent behind the question "What is my best purpose?"

We usually ask this because we are unsatisfied with our lives on some level and within this question we would like the answer to be given in terms that apply to our own personal agenda, whether that agenda involves the making of money, spiritual enlightenment or helping others. If there is no specific goal present when we ask ourselves this question, then we are asking purely on an emotional level and the emotion is giving direction to the question. So perhaps this is not the best time to ask!

If at this moment in time you are interested in finding your purpose, try to answer (honestly) the following three questions:

1.      Are you asking the question "What is my best purpose in life?" because you are dissatisfied with some aspect of your life?

2.      If you were totally satisfied and happy with every aspect of your life would you still ask yourself the question "What is my best purpose in life?"

3.      When you ask yourself the question "What is my best purpose in life?" do you have a particular agenda in mind? For instance, would you like to have more money, are you materialistically driven, would you like to help others, etc?

I believe that most people, if they were totally happy with

their lives, would not ask the question in the first place. Normally everyone has their own personal agenda or specific reasons behind wanting to find their true purpose. These statements, I'm sure, may be completely obvious to most. However because we have to use specific terminology when talking to the Higher Self or even the subconscious mind, we must firstly clearly define the motivation behind wanting to ask the question "What is my best purpose in life?"

So firstly, look at what it is you really want in your life, ask yourself why you want this and then define it further. If it's not done in this way, then the Higher Self will not be able to respond correctly. For example, do you really want to find your best purpose in life or do you just want to be emotionally fulfilled, or physically fulfilled, (financially or otherwise)?. Establish your agenda before you convert your statement into a question. Otherwise it is possible to create a conflict within yourself which may result in anxiety and could even make your situation worse.

When we ask to find our best purpose we may be actually asking for something or someone on some level to help make us feel happy and loved. So if you need to feel emotionally fulfilled, then this is what you should ask for instead of the 'purpose' question. Hopefully, when you have studied your personal feelings in depth, you will be able to find out whether you truly want to find your purpose or whether you simply want to feel loved and fulfilled. If this is what you really want, then ask for it! (Don't create a conflict within by asking your Higher Self to provide something that you don't really want or need).

If you really want to know your true purpose, then you must ask the question in the following way using the Em-Power Disc:

*"Give me what I need and make me become completely aware of my best purpose in this life, as soon as possible, starting now".*

We say 'as soon as possible' instead of 'now' because what you are asking for is not a physical response, but a shift in awareness that will allow your individual best purpose to become crystal clear in your mind. Certain situations and events may need to occur in order for that to happen, but by giving this specific command you are in a sense setting a ball in motion, which will ultimately lead to the answer to this question.

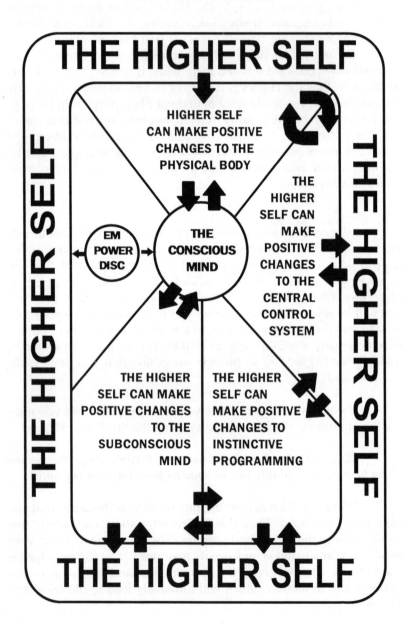

# INTELLIGENT ENERGY

Einstein stated that $E=mc^2$. This equation says that energy is matter and matter is energy and all things therefore are made up of energy. For example, one gram of matter (including the human organism) is equal to 25,000,000 kilowatts of energy. Consider for one moment the possibility of energy itself being a form of intelligence. We see evidence of this intelligence everywhere in nature and science. If we assume that energy is intelligent and that all matter is a physical manifestation of this intelligent energy, it opens the door to an entirely new way of thinking.

How clever is your pen? It is made up of molecules of energy in a particular structure and you are able to use this energy to create letters, draw pictures, etc. As we discussed earlier, energy and matter may appear different, but they are in fact one and the same thing, matter being merely energy in a specific state or configuration.

Obviously, physical things are easier for us to relate to, but not many of us will think of the glass of water we are drinking, the glass and the water itself, as energy in a physical form. Most of us relate to energy as something like an electrical force or a 'glowing' yellow ball, or possibly a laser beam. But release the energy in the tip of a pinhead and you would more than likely cause an explosion! Atomic energy is released in this way.

Every plant, every tree, every piece of vegetation that exists, is made up of this intelligent energy. We can mix various herbs and plants together and create remedies for illnesses. But consider that each ingredient that we use is in fact intelligent energy, and as we pick different intelligent energies and bring them together, in a sense they become clever enough to heal anything!

Consider the possibility that this intelligent energy is in fact a code, and that the code represents the formula in which the energy exists, either a tree, a cup, or a blade of grass. The human biological organism is constructed of complex sequences of energy, which will produce a person when brought together. The information that creates these sequences is housed in our instinctive programming. For the purpose of this book we will refer to these intelligent energies as 'energy codes'. In order for you to visualise the way in which these codes work, try to imagine each code being like a word made up of both vowels and consonants. Every word has an initial route. Let's take the word 'climb' for instance. From the route word 'climb', we can move forward with 'climbing', or 'climbed' or 'climber'. Adding letters such as 'ing', 'ed' or 'er' will change the sense of the word.

All intelligent energy contains these base 'route' codes with many additional variations, which, if applied, would totally alter the form in which energy manifests itself, from a living organism to your teacup! Your teacup may contain several route codes which could be identical to the route codes found within a human energy system, but that wouldn't make a person a cup! *(See diagram, "Intelligent Energy", page 114).*

Every law in nature (such as gravity) is made up of energy codes. If we were to drop a ball from a height of ten metres, the weight of the ball and the distance would determine the velocity and force on impact with the ground. It is as if gravity imposes its energy codes onto the ball's energy codes and the result is quantifiable in mathematics. Unless you have a degree in quantum physics or a doctorate in mathematics, you will probably find the intricacies of energy codes rather daunting. Perhaps one day we may discover a way of recording them. If this were the case, then we could possibly use them to generate or alter the energy code sequencing, which would enable energy to become literally anything we want - from a cup, to a tree, to a blade of grass, or possibly a new heart or organ which could be transplanted. But, at present, these codes are beyond the grasp of our society. Perhaps when we are ready we will discover the very foundation of life and the universe!

As far as the Em-Power Disc is concerned, it merely gives one the ability to enhance and manipulate energy codes within the body and mind, to help re-route, clarify and improve our physical and mental well-being.

The energy within the body could be described as a river leading to the sea. Imagine that where the river begins, rain clouds are blown by winds across the land and as they find higher cooler ground they release rain. This rain is sent by gravity on a journey back to its source. Firstly it finds a stream, then it becomes a river, which may take precarious courses through twists and turns, but eventually it will find its way back to the sea.

Our energy systems are like a river, each leading to a different sea and finding the best way to reach various destinations around the body. As with a river, if suddenly a rock or landslide alters the terrain, a blockage may occur. As the pressure of the water increases due to the blockage one of three things may happen. The sheer pressure of the water may remove the rock itself, the water may take an alternative route, or perhaps the river will burst its banks and flood the surrounding countryside. We have already noted that in our body's energy systems, blockages may occur due to structural or emotional damage. These blockages may cause a lack of communication within the body, resulting in the inability of the body to correct itself. Unless the blockage is removed or redirected, many problems will remain or deteriorate, or perhaps even spread to other areas.

# ENERGY BALANCING

All the systems in the body are designed to work in unison so that we can maintain what is known as homeostasis (keeping the body's internal conditions constant). For example, if we are confronted with cold weather conditions then naturally we shiver. This shivering action automatically increases our temperature and this is the way the body tries to regulate itself. The same principle applies to every aspect of our physical being.

To ensure that all our systems can collaborate and also respond quickly to any situation, it is very important that the energy flow around the body is maintained. Any reduction in energy flow will result in decreasing response times, making us prone to illness and susceptible to climatic conditions. One of the main functions of the Em-Power Disc is to help boost the energy field thus enhancing the communication process within the body.

# THE FIVE AURA LAYERS

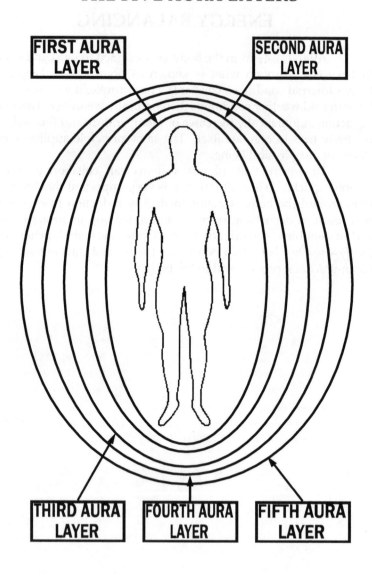

FIRST AURA LAYER

SECOND AURA LAYER

THIRD AURA LAYER

FOURTH AURA LAYER

FIFTH AURA LAYER

# THE AURA

An aura is a field of energy that emanates from all living things. Biblical drawings often depict angelic scenes where spiritual beings have rings of light floating six inches above their heads. These rings of light are often depicted as golden halos.

With the advent of Kirlian photography, (a unique method of filming the colours of the aura), auras have been found to exist around all matter. As with so many other unexplained mysteries, science has discovered a method to observe and explain the aura. Until the moment science found a way to record this phenomena, it considered claims of its existence to be nothing other than ridiculous. It is ironic how the crackpot theories of ancient wisdom eventually become real undisputed scientific fact.

## *AURA LIGHT THEORY*

Auras are energetic representations of who and what we are. They reflect every aspect of our physical, emotional and spiritual state of being. The aura is like a Russian doll, made up of layer upon layer of representational images, which mirror a central core. Kirlian photography can only pick up a specific spectrum of these layered formations, but however spectacular these photographs may appear to be they do not fully represent the phenomena. It is similar to comparing a black and white photograph of actors performing in a play with the experience of being in the theatre and watching the play itself. With the photograph, only a fraction can be appreciated. The whole picture is a wondrous visual and sensory experience.

Some people are able to see and experience auras, depending on their natural abilities. To some extent this ability can be taught and developed. I can try and describe the process of observation that is needed to see auras. It is quite simply the 'way' in which we look at something; an attempt to investigate and look beyond what we would normally be aware or conscious of.

It is like looking into a crack or small hole in a wall. At a distance you will only see the outline of the crack, but if you went closer you may begin to see light emanating from the other side of the crack. If you were to take a couple of steps more, you would see glimpses of movement behind the crack, and if you came up really close you would be able to make out shapes of people and objects on the other side. But if you put your eye right up to the crack, you would see everything. If you put your ear to the wall you could hear things. You could even smell the roses in the garden behind the wall, by putting your nose to the crack and breathing in the air. Some people may look at the wall from a distance and never even notice the crack, or it may take another person to point out the crack in the wall before they become aware of it. Then it's actually up to you and your curiosity to discover what's on the other side.

# THE LAYERS OF THE AURA
*(See diagram, page 118)*

## *LAYER ONE (THE BLUEPRINT OF LIFE)*

The colour of this layer is gold. This layer is a representation, which depicts individual perfection on all levels - physical, mental, emotional and spiritual. It is as if we exist as perfect beings within shells of imperfection. Imagine this aura being like a brand new white suit - clean and bright. As we go through life this suit gets dirty and needs cleaning. We must simply remove the extra dirt, which is in fact accumulated negative programming, and it will become like new again. Many healers intentionally concentrate on cleaning the aura as part of their therapy. This aura is the representation of your Higher Self and your connection with God.

Michelangelo was once asked to explain how he could produce such magnificent statues from the very difficult medium of marble. He thought for a while and said, "It's very simple, I go to the quarry, find a piece of marble I like, place it on a table, remove all the pieces I don't need and the statue appears". In other words, we are all pieces of marble, in which a beautiful statue exists, just waiting for the unnecessary bits to be removed! The ultimate goal of spiritual awareness is to become the beautiful statue that exists within.

## *THE SECOND LAYER (INSTINCTIVE PROGRAMMING)*

This layer is usually pale yellow in colour and represents our genetic and environmental programming (instinctive programming). This programming has been passed down from one generation to the other, with all its strong character traits like kindness, ego, fear and hope. Often a sensitive healer can feel this instinctive programming.

Your mother or father may have a specific physical or emotional characteristic such as a bad back or a quick temper - it could be literally anything. These weaknesses or attributes can be represented in your aura field. You may or may not develop the same trait, but there is a good chance that you might. In some cases, this aura field is so strong that a healer can personally experience the problem while in contact with the patient to the point where they may feel their pain, or the pain of another member of their family.

In many cases it is best to try to heal any negative character trait before it has chance to manifest itself. Many people also believe in past lives, which may be a part of our instinctive programming. This is an entirely different subject, but often an unresolved past life experience, can lead to present life anxieties. Healing this problem, whether we believe in it or not, can sometimes help.

Your brain is constantly updating this second aura level according to your personal experiences. As this aura level is being manipulated by our thought patterns and in-built programming, it can vary depending on what information we feed through to our subconscious through the five senses.

## *THE THIRD LEVEL (THE PHYSICAL FIELD).*

This is the strongest of all the aura levels and with Kirlian photography we can actually see this aura layer. Often these pictures show very energetic physical energies, which look like piercing blue, white, red, yellow, neon lights emanating from and around our bodies. Healers often have a very strong physical energy field and in tests the Kirlien photography confirms this.

This aura layer is a representation of the communication between the various parts of the body. The complex energy patterns it creates are messages being sent to each and every cell. An energy pattern is like a list of instructions that tells each cell in the body what its function is. If these energy messages are blocked or slowed down, then the content of the instructions within the message can lead to misinterpretation, which ultimately may lead to a malfunction. If the energy blockage is detected by the central control system, it will register a malfunction and send out a repair message to release the blockage in the problem area. Pain is a message that is sent from this self-corrective system to tell the conscious mind to change its behaviour in order to protect the problem area until it has had a chance to heal itself.

For example, if you twist your ankle, it will produce a pain signal, which will alter your behaviour in such a way that you do not put pressure on the ankle until it has healed. You know that the ankle is healing as the pain eases.

Using the Em-Power Disc can speed up this process by amplifying the messages being sent by the central control system to correct a problem. As we give an instruction in the form of a command sequence to the Higher Self, the Higher Self will respond by creating a programme for the body and mind to follow. The Higher Self, via our energy field (the aura) then transmits this programme to the body and mind.

Sometimes it is necessary to give this new energy field a helping hand to reach its destination. Imagine that these energy fields are travelling down wires. If there is an accidental break in the wire, the message will not reach its destination. To repair the damage and complete the circuit we must link the broken wires together again. Some people's energy fields are capable of acting like jump leads that connect the circuit. Conventional 'hands on' healing often works in this way. The problem however, is that the circuitry between two people is not always compatible because one may operate at a slightly different 'voltage' or 'frequency' to another. As the Em-Power Disc contains multiple communication frequencies, it is possible to use it as the connector by placing it on the problem area.

## THE FOURTH LEVEL (EMOTIONAL)

This is a very large field that emanates a great distance in all directions from the body. The colour of this aura level depends on the mood or emotional state of a person. For example, gold indicates serenity and peace. Violet indicates a searching for emotional and spiritual awareness. Red indicates unresolved emotional situations. Blue indicates an expanding consciousness, a willingness to learn and positive creation. It is very rare that you will see just one colour: usually the emotional aura is a combination of many different colours.

Each colour is displayed as part of a whole picture. Imagine for a moment, a beautiful sunset. The general mood of the picture can vary greatly according to the many colours it contains. The most dominant colour sets the general tone for the scene and the rest is left to interpretation depending on the proportion and intensity of the colours in relation to the whole picture. It is like this with the fourth emotional aura level. It can take time and experience to correctly interpret these complex emotional representations, but patience and practice are the key words.

# THE FIFTH LEVEL
# (THE COSMIC CONNECTION)

This is the level at which we connect to other living things. This aura level looks like a beam of light, which emanates from the crown of the head, although sometimes it can also appear at other specific energy points, called chakras. It looks like a vortex, or a funnel-shaped spinning column. Imagine this vortex, made up of energy, spiralling upwards from the crown area and outwards from the chakras.

We all have this cosmic connection, although some people are more connected than others. This is the doorway to the universal mind consciousness. All the knowledge of the universe is said to exist within this 'cosmic internet'. When this doorway is opened a person feels a bonding with all living things: a combination of joy, love and infinity. Within this doorway, time and space have no meaning. The past, present and future are as one. Astral projection is the ability to step through this doorway and ride the currents that ebb and flow through time and space.

In summary, the aura field is a representation of our energy and spiritual selves. It emanates from the body and radiates in layers. Each layer has a significant purpose but interacts with the whole, in a similar way to the body's known systems, which interact with each other to maintain a correct balance.

Early experiments with the Em-Power Disc using Kirlian photography suggest that the user's energy or aura field is greatly enhanced, expanded and put in balance. In Em-Power Therapy there are specific command sequences that you can give to your Higher Self which will trigger the spontaneous cleaning and balancing of the aura field.

# THE CHAKRAS

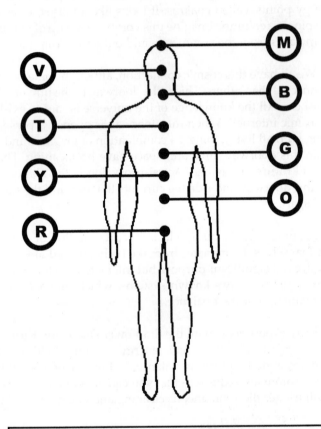

| M | = | MAGENTA | THE CROWN |
| V | = | VIOLET | THE FOREHEAD |
| B | = | BLUE | THE THROAT |
| T | = | TURQUOISE | THE THYMUS |
| G | = | GREEN | THE HEART |
| Y | = | YELLOW | THE SOLAR PLEXUS |
| O | = | ORANGE | THE STOMACH |
| R | = | RED | THE BASE CHAKRA |

# COLOUR THERAPY AND THE CHAKRAS

The power of colours to affect our mood and emotional state is well known. An entire therapy known as colour therapy has been developed to use the influence of colour to heal the physical, emotional and spiritual self. In traditional colour therapy, each colour represents an energy centre around the body that is known as a 'chakra'. These energy centres lie along a vertical line from the crown of the head down the body. Each colour represents an aspect of the physical, emotional and spiritual self.

When a chakra is said to be weak then a person is prone to certain problems associated with the physical, emotional or spiritual aspects of that area. For example, the colour representing the chakra located at the solar plexus is yellow. As this chakra is associated with certain aspects and characteristics, if there is a weakness here in an individual, then emotionally they may fall prone to such things as insecurity which may fuel a desire to take control, or a lack of focus and involvement.

## *THE CHAKRAS* (See diagram, page 124)

**(M) The crown chakra is MAGENTA.** This area is responsible for raising energy levels. It represents the centre of our spiritual growth, self-respect, dignity and self-composure. When properly in balance we feel 'at peace' with ourselves. When out of balance we can feel as if we have a lack of control over our surroundings, experience feelings of low self-esteem and find it difficult to concentrate properly. We may easily lose our self-composure altogether. The Magenta or Crown chakra represents the upper brain, pineal gland and right eye.

**(V) The chakra located at the forehead is VIOLET.** It represents peace, love, individuality and inner balance. When this chakra is out of balance we can feel tense, anxious and insecure. We may experience a loss of identity and have difficulty with concentration. This chakra represents the lower brain, left eye, pituitary gland and ears, nose and central nervous system.

**(B) The throat chakra is SKY BLUE** and is the balancing centre for the body's metabolism. When this chakra is out of balance we can feel stressed, anxious and tense and we are unable to communicate properly with others. It represents the thyroid, throat, bronchial and vocal systems and the lungs.

**(T) The chakra located at the thymus or breastbone is TURQUOISE.**
This chakra is the centre for positive thought and communication processes within the body. When it is out of balance it can cause tension, anxiety, lack of perceived control of one's physical body and negative thought processes. It represents the thymus and is associated with a healthy immune system and the production of antibodies.

**(G) The heart chakra is GREEN** and it is our emotional balancing centre. When this chakra is out of balance our emotional equilibrium can become unstable and we may feel disorientated and confused. It can interfere with our decision-making process and possibly develop a fear of open spaces. It is responsible for the heart, blood, vagus nerve and circulatory systems. We can often use this energy centre in conjunction with the Em-Power Disc to access and communicate with other systems in the body and connect us with the Higher Self.

**(Y) The chakra located at the solar plexus is YELLOW.** As previously stated, when this chakra is out of balance we can feel insecure and have a need to take control. We can also experience a lack of involvement and focus. On a physical level it can cause nervousness, tension, confusion and lack of orientation. It is responsible for the pancreas, stomach, liver, gall bladder and the nervous system.

**(O) The chakra located at the stomach is ORANGE.** It is responsible for the release and production of energy and digestion. When it is out of balance we can feel physically insecure, develop a resentment of authority, are prone to stress and can suffer from irritable bowel syndrome. It is responsible for the spleen and reproductive systems.

**(R) The base chakra, located at the bottom of the spine, is RED.** Traditionally it is viewed as the 'seat for the life-force' and is responsible for vitality and self-expression. When this chakra is out of balance you can feel exhausted, oppressed, stressed and physically weak. It is responsible for the adrenals, spinal column and kidneys.

# ANCIENT WISDOM

Many Eastern and ancient philosophies acknowledge the chakras as being the spiritual centres of the body. The number of chakras can vary from six to twelve depending on the particular tradition. Visually the chakras can look like energy spirals or vortexes, which some people can actually see, and may contain more than one colour. Some people view the chakras as being like flowers with their petals opening to display the spirituality and energy of our being.

There is a very powerful visualisation that anyone can use to try and open up or unblock the chakras. Imagine a lovely flower, such as a sunflower for example and visualise this flower, with its petals closed on any one of your chakra points. Slowly feed the flower with your energy and as you do this, picture the petals opening one by one.

With the Em-Power Disc, we are able to cleanse, unblock and restore all of the chakras using specifically constructed command sequences.

## *UNBLOCKING ENERGY POINTS*

To maintain the body's equilibrium it is important that our energy pathways do not become blocked. Should such a blockage occur it will slow down the healing process and many of the natural communication processes in the body. Many techniques, including acupuncture, acupressure and Ayur Veda, use methods that are specifically designed to remove and release any energy block that may occur in the body.

Through our studies we have found that acupuncture can be a very successful means. But it can take many years to learn the process and it can be expensive and/or inconvenient to visit an acupuncturist each time you develop a blockage in one of your energy pathways. So we have developed a relatively simple method by which you can use your Em-Power Disc to release an energy block.

By simply placing a Disc on specific points of the body for approximately one minute you will remove most blockages in the body. It is always best to ask a friend or member of your family to unblock your energy system, rather than attempting to do it yourself. Often it can be awkward to place the Disc on certain points without getting physically tangled! This in itself would restrict the flow of energy around your body.

## THE CYCLE OF LIFE

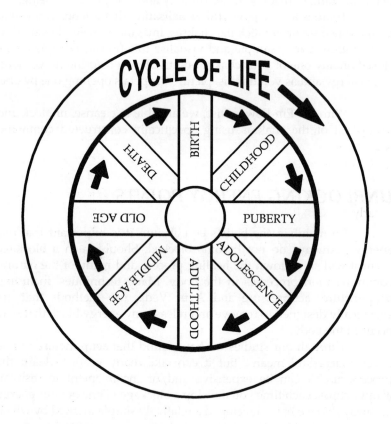

# THE CYCLE PRINCIPLE

The Cycle Principle states that every living thing is dependent on many cycles for it to exist.

Every physical, mental, emotional and spiritual aspect of ourselves is subject to the Cycle Principle. It is a process that applies to every living cell in our body, every thought that we have and every aspect of our entire being.

What is a cycle in simple terms? It is the process of birth, growth and death. Our instinctive programming, which we can define as being inherited information passed on through the generations, determines the function and purpose of each cycle within our body, mind and spirit.

Within an individual cycle there are three basic components:
**FORMATION, ACTION AND COMPLETION.**

**FORMATION** is the beginning of a cycle. Our instinctive programming determines the basic function, purpose and nature of this process. Once a cycle has been formed, its function and purpose is clearly defined and the cycle principle is set into motion.

**ACTION** is the direction and physical attributes of a cycle. In other words it is 'what actually happens' during the cycle's lifetime.

**COMPLETION** is the termination of an action within the cycle. Often after the completion of a cycle, it is renewed and the process will repeat itself.

Let's look at a prime example of the Cycle Principle. The cycle of 'life' is birth, childhood, puberty, adolescence, adulthood, middle age, old age and death (*see diagram, page 128*). We can describe the cycle of life as being like a wheel that rotates in a clockwise direction. All other cycles within the body, mind and spirit are merely 'wheels within wheels'.

Each moment, depending on where we are within the cycle of life, there are literally millions of cycles dying and being reborn within our body and mind. Although many cycles are predetermined by our instinctive programming they can be influenced by the way we feel and the situations and events that make up our day-to-day lives. We can create our own positive and negative cycles (especially those associated with the subconscious mind), through our life experiences and the way we perceive and interpret them. A very strong negative-

*THE CYCLE PRINCIPLE*

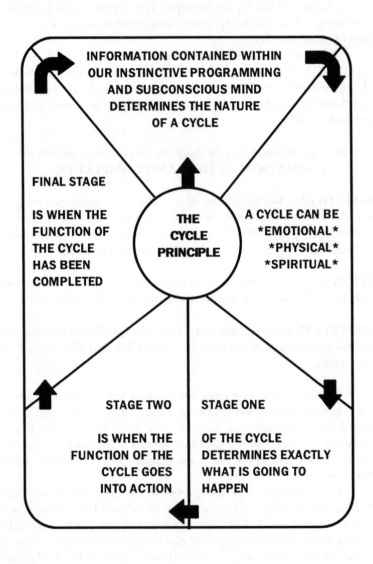

INFORMATION CONTAINED WITHIN
OUR INSTINCTIVE PROGRAMMING
AND SUBCONSCIOUS MIND
DETERMINES THE NATURE
OF A CYCLE

**FINAL STAGE**

**IS WHEN THE
FUNCTION OF
THE CYCLE
HAS BEEN
COMPLETED**

THE
CYCLE
PRINCIPLE

**A CYCLE CAN BE
*EMOTIONAL*
*PHYSICAL*
*SPIRITUAL***

**STAGE TWO**

**IS WHEN THE
FUNCTION OF THE
CYCLE GOES
INTO ACTION**

**STAGE ONE**

**OF THE CYCLE
DETERMINES EXACTLY
WHAT IS GOING TO
HAPPEN**

ly perceived event could have a detrimental impact on many different cycles within the body and mind. Such a situation can often be a catalyst for malfunction and disease.

It is possible to make long-term, positive changes to a cycle if we can pinpoint exactly when it was formed. It is only at the formation stage that a cycle is vulnerable to either positive or negative change. Fortunately this vulnerability is limited to a brief time frame which is anything from 6 to 24 hours within an average 28 to 30 day period. In other words, a specific cycle can only be changed if we have a powerful life experience during a precise 24-hour period in any 28 to 30 day cycle. In Em-Power Therapy we call this period of vulnerability the 'Cycle Impact Zone'. If a powerful negative situation occurs, such as a loved one dying, precisely at the time of a cycle impact zone, it can have a detrimental effect on a person's health and well-being. These negative effects could stay with the person throughout their entire life if they do not make the necessary changes. Therefore knowledge and understanding of our cycle impact zones can be life enhancing.

By communicating with your Higher Self through the Em-Power Disc it is possible to examine a cycle and find its impact zone. Armed with this information you are then able to make radical positive changes to your physical, mental and emotional well-being.

Let's look at the various kinds of cycles that exist within the body, mind and spirit and see how we can use the knowledge we have gained from communicating with the Higher Self to make long-term positive changes on all levels. *(See diagram, "The Cycle Principle", page 130).*

What are the most important cycles that affect us in our everyday lives?

**PHYSICAL, MENTAL, EMOTIONAL, SPIRITUAL, INHERITED.**

What are the main things that can affect, influence or change the nature of a cycle within a cycle impact zone?

*A perceived sense of loss (such as the death of a loved one)*
*A physical trauma (such as an accident)*
*Unnecessary conditioning (by parents, society, religion, etc.)*
*Environmental conditions (where we live for example, pollution, etc.)*
*Life experiences contained within the subconscious mind (e.g. powerful childhood situations).*

Literally any powerful or emotional experience that occurs within a cycle impact zone can have an influence on a cycle. If a serious change to a specific cycle occurs, it can affect many different interconnected cycles. For example, if you are the kind of person that has fluctuating weight, it could be that a powerful and emotional experience happened to you as a child, precisely on a cycle impact zone. This experience would have initially only affected your emotional cycle, but left unchecked it may have eventually influenced and changed your metabolic cycle, inner child cycle and possibly many other physical and emotional cycles. Ultimately it is possible that such an event could eventually change your instinctive programming and unwittingly you could pass this cycle on, with all its consequences, to your children.

The advantage of knowing the precise nature of a cycle impact zone is that you can make life-enhancing changes to the very nature of the cycles within you. In fact you could reverse the effects of negative inherited cycles coming from your instinctive programming. These positive changes could include optimum health, high-speed learning and increased intellectual capacity. The key to achieving these positive changes involves communicating with your Higher Self.

## HOW DO WE MAKE POSITIVE CHANGES TO A CYCLE USING EM-POWER THERAPY?

As the Higher Self can influence or change the nature of a cycle by establishing two-way communication with the Higher Self you can:

*Find out the precise date and time of a specific cycle impact zone
*Determine if a cycle is responsible for a negative situation
*Discover if any other cycles have been affected by an event in the past
*Discover whether a specific negative cycle is coming from your Instinctive Programming.
After analysing the above information you can then use specifically worded command sequences to:
*Change the negative components within a cycle and thus influence the outcome from negative to positive
*Remove any triggers responsible for the perpetuation of a negative cycle
*Adjust the polarity of the energy from negative to positive within the

*body, mind and spirit in order to increase your energy levels*
*\*Create new cycles that can increase life expectancy and dramatically improve your health*
*\*Create your own personal 'Cycle Chart' that includes the impact zones of the cycles that influence you the most*
*\*Avoid negative situations that can affect a cycle.*

Over a year ago, a lady called Maureen came to see me. She had been suffering flu-type symptoms and chest infections, which had been re-occurring over a three-month period. She had been prescribed drugs such as antibiotics from her doctor, but they had had little or no effect. We activated the Em-Power Disc and by communicating with her Higher Self identified the cycle impact zone of her emotional cycle.

After we had determined the precise formation date of her emotional cycle, (which was approximately three months previously), we discovered that on this exact day her mother, who was greatly loved, had died at the age of 92. Because this had occurred during Maureen's emotional cycle impact zone it had triggered a series of physical responses. In this instance we told her Higher Self to remove any negative triggers associated with her emotional cycle and within a few days Maureen was feeling much better. One year later however, on the anniversary of her mother's death, the emotion was re-triggered and Maureen's symptoms started again. Therefore, especially at our most vulnerable times, we may need to repeat this process to permanently remove any ongoing negative physical side effects.

As you can see, timing is crucial when it comes to making positive changes in the body and mind. Often we will not decide to make positive life changes until something really bad happens. A special kind of survival cycle can be triggered during times of our greatest despair and anxiety. I call this the 'last resort cycle'; as for many people it is a lifesaver and can turn their lives around. The last resort cycle is created by our instinctive programming and without it we would probably give up in very difficult situations.

In summary, cycles and their impact zones play a crucial role in our everyday lives and if a negative situation or event occurs during an impact zone we are vulnerable on many levels (emotional, physical and spiritual). Em-Power Therapy, however, can give you an easy to use method of establishing and correcting a negative physical or emotional condition which is a result of an event that has occurred during a cycle impact zone.

134

# SYMBOLS AND SYMBOLISM

From biblical times to the present day, symbols and symbolism have played a crucial part in the communication process between people. In many cases they have been the trigger or cause of the formation of a specific language. Egyptian hieroglyphics are a good example of the way in which symbols can be used to convey intent or information.

Symbols are often representations of our surroundings and in their original form may have looked like a simple line drawing such as a tree, house, temple, etc. These drawings eventually formed a rudimentary language. The reason why symbols have very powerful meanings is contained within our instinctive programming. Religious symbols in particular have tremendous power for people of that specific faith or denomination, to the extent where a symbol can be a catalyst for healing, given the right set of environmental circumstances.

These symbols act as triggers for our instinctive programming. Whereas the subconscious mind contains the sum of our experiences, our instinctive programming contains information with very highly charged emotional content (passed down from generation to generation). A symbol can have a positive, negative or neutral effect on an individual. It may appear absolutely meaningless to one person, and yet to another it may trigger a profound physical, emotional or spiritual experience.

There is no real uniformity to the experiences between individuals as one person's response to a symbol is often totally different to that of another. The incredible thing about the Em-Power Disc is that it allows us all to see and experience the power of symbols in a uniformed way. This means that if one person feels happy when looking at a specific symbol while wearing the Disc, the next person will also feel the same basic emotion when looking at the same symbol. The Disc is no exception to all other communication devices in the sense that it operates using a language of sorts, only this language is the language of the Higher Self.

Most healing techniques operate using a simplistic language of a kind. In acupuncture, for example, it is the language of 'points' where a specific set of co-ordinates are designed to trigger certain responses within the individual. This is a language in itself. Reiki uses symbolism a great deal to send different energy frequencies for healing. These symbols are highly prized and given to the individual after an initiation ceremony. However bizarre this ritual may appear to some, this initiation plays a big part in most religious cultures and even university fraternities (particularly in the USA) have some kind of initiation ceremony when new students join a specific group. The initiation process has been passed down from master/teacher to student and it is really only the handing over of information from one to another. The ceremony, in a sense, intensifies and symbolises the importance of the information being passed to the student. For obvious reasons, if we feel that something has great value we learn to treasure it more and more. Giving value to this information in passing it to others is probably only a psychological process but it is nevertheless crucial. It is said that knowledge is power and in our world this is very true, for the more we know and understand about our world then the more we can use what we know to our advantage.

Numbers are also symbols of a kind. They represent a unit of measurement and are being used by scientists world-wide to unravel the meaning of the universe. The recent book 'The Bible Code' by Michael Drosning, and the renowned world class mathematician Dr.Eliyahu Rips, have both caused international controversy. 'The Bible Code' claims that, contained within the Old Testament, in the original language of Hebrew, there is a type of computer programme, which can now be read using a mathematical formula and modern technology. This has naturally caused a stir, as the information within the Old Testament is said to be more than 3000 years old and yet this programme can accurately predict events that have occurred throughout history. The discovery of this technical and futuristic information encoded in something so ancient and established is a little hard to take in. It is more incredible than, say, finding a spaceship buried under a pyramid!

We have mapped out our world and have taken journeys to the stars but the greatest mysteries on earth are yet to be revealed. Perhaps instead of spaceships and boats, we will turn our attention to the microcosm, where the smallest of the small will unravel the workings of the Universe. These journeys will be taken in the fullness of time, but we will use mathematical equations to travel the world of the microcosm. Many of Einstein's equations were not established for several years and it is only over time that we can prove or disprove anything. However, equations do tend to prove themselves to be correct or incorrect, and once proved remain relatively constant.

# THE EM-POWER WHEEL OF SPIRITUALITY DIAGRAM

*"The Em-Power Wheel as a whole is designed
to fulfil a specific purpose "*

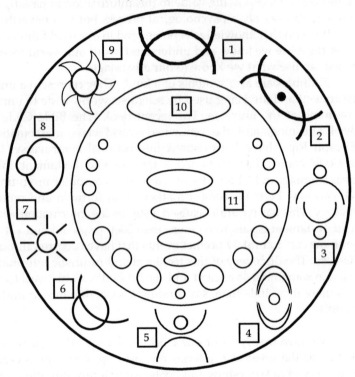

SYMBOLS KEY
1  = STARTING POINT (POWERING UP)
2  = HIGHER SELF CONNECTION
3  = UNITY OF MIND AND BODY
4  = REPRESENTS YOUR PERSONAL CONCEPT OF GOD
5  = HOLY
6  = THE DIVINE
7  = POSITIVE ENERGY
8  = REMOVAL OF NEGATIVE SPIRITUAL CYCLES
9  = REPRESENTS THE "TIME FRAME" ASPECT OF THE COMMAND
    SEQUENCES "NOW"
10 = SETS OF CO-ORDINATES OR INSTRUCTIONS TELLING THE BODY THE
    SPECIFIC AREAS THAT NEED UNBLOCKING.
11 = CENTRE OR "NUCLEUS" COLOUR REPRESENTS THE MAIN CHAKRA
    ASSOCIATED WITH THE PRIMARY FUNCTION OF THE WHEEL.

# THE EM-POWER WHEEL

Em-Power Therapy shows the individual various ways of communicating with the Higher Self and it has designed a system of visual communication which is based on symbols *(See diagram "The Em-Power Wheel", page 136)*. They are designed like wheels that rotate in a clockwise direction.

Each symbol contained within the outer edge of the wheel represents an individual instruction, command or statement and together they are designed to fulfil a specific purpose, such as the removal of anxiety or fear. In fact, the symbols on the wheel represent and replace the command sequences and instructions we give to our body, so the order of these instructions is important. This is why we work clockwise around the wheel starting at the 12 o'clock position.

The centre (or nucleus) colour represents the main chakra that is associated with the primary function of the wheel (magenta, violet, blue, turquoise, green, yellow, orange, and red). For example, the colour Magenta represents the chakra associated with spiritual development, so an Em-Power Wheel with a magenta centre would primarily have a spiritual function. The small coloured dots within the nucleus are sets of co-ordinates or instructions, which tell the body the specific areas that need unblocking (in a similar way to the position of the needles in acupuncture).

Every Em-Power Wheel has a particular function. For example, it could be to correct a specific physical problem, developing or improving spiritual and psychic awareness, or conquering fears and phobias. Each wheel requires a certain amount of energy to properly activate the appropriate command sequences and the amount of energy we use depends on the function of each wheel.

The symbols used in Em-Power Therapy are not visual representations of the function itself (for example, the symbol for 'happiness' is not a smiling face) and so cannot be construed as a suggestion of any kind. Often the simplest of symbols are the most powerful. Em-Power Therapy is designed to teach us how to use symbols to help achieve our goals.

# THE EM-POWER DISC

The communication processes within the body are far more sophisticated than we can really imagine. Each system in the body uses its own language to communicate with another system, sending out millions of messages every second, and that language is as unique as a fingerprint. Imagine for one moment that we had the knowledge to perform a brain transplant. We may find that it would take years for the new brain to discover all the communication processes of its new body, because one person's brain and body may have a totally different language to the next!

If a patient had to have an organ transplant, the doctors would have to find a donor with the same blood type to try to make the best match possible because the more perfect the match from the donor to the recipient, the less chance there is of rejection of the organ. Again, the reason for this is that the cells of the organ from the donor are different to the cells of the recipient. Eventually the receiving body learns to communicate properly with the new organ, which results in it functioning correctly. Such is the complexity of the communication systems within the body.

Let's just say that we wanted to install a new programme into our computer - it could be something simple like a new spell check. If this programme wasn't designed for our computer's specific operating system, then our computer won't accept it. We can do one of two things. Either we can change the machine and its operating system, or buy a new programme that is compatible with our computer.

Now imagine we have a special universal device designed to be used by any computer system in existence. We could add this to our computer and once activated it would allow our machine to accept and use any programme. In a sense, this device is a universal translator. It is in this way that we should think about the Em-Power Disc. Think of it as being a special and unique device that the energy field of the body can read. In simple terms, this is how it works:

The Disc is placed within a person's energy field. The energy field reads the information contained on the Disc. This information teaches the body how to access a new level of communication: the universal translator. This new level of communication makes it possible to have an interactive conversation with the different parts of the body and mind. We can literally talk to it for the first time and tell it what we would like it to do.

People frequently ask me, when they first come into contact with the Em-Power Disc, what it is that I do to enable a little piece of aluminium to work in this way. It is very difficult to give a credible scientific explanation, as the processes involved in the Disc's manufacture are a combination of 'thought form theory' and my unusual abilities. For some, this explanation isn't enough, and they perceive that there is 'something else' included in the process which for some reason I am not prepared to disclose. This initial apprehension or scepticism will sometimes stop certain people from even trying Em-Power Therapy.

In my experience however, if a person has a physical problem or is perhaps interested in the subject of self-healing, they will try the Disc and often will have incredible experiences which do lead to self-healing. Or at least they will receive the physical or practical proof that they need to clearly demonstrate the benefits of using Em-Power Therapy. This physical, practical proof of the phenomenon behind the Em-Power Disc is what usually persuades those few people who are initially reluctant to try it, or are very sceptical at first.

The main function of the Em-Power Disc is to allow a person to have an interactive conversation with their Higher Self through their physical body. The Higher Self of the individual can answer many of the questions that I am unable to answer at this time anyway. These answers can be in the form of a simple 'yes' or 'no', or they can be a more sophisticated sense of 'knowing', understanding and eventual acceptance. However this communication is made, the advantages to the individual are potentially immeasurable. The positive uses of the Em-Power Disc as an interactive communication device are so overwhelming that they mostly override any sceptical misgivings of the individual or the need to understand precisely how it works in scientific terms.

One of the main purposes of the Em-Power Research Programme is to try to discover the science behind how the Disc works. We realise that this may take many years. We view the phenomenon as something similar to the discovery of electricity, which was initially inexplicable but eventually science was able to unravel its mystery.

The Em-Power Disc is a piece of anodised aluminium 35mm in diameter. Through our research we have discovered a way of affecting the energy contained within the molecules of the aluminium, which allows us to store information onto the Em-Power Disc. The possibility that another individual or company could identify, reproduce or manufacture an equivalent product would be as unlikely as winning the lottery every week for the next one hundred years! All Em-Power Discs have a registered trademark and we would caution anyone to be aware of possible pirating or other products making similar claims.

To prevent exploitation and fraud to members of the public who wish to use the Em-Power Disc, several security factors have been employed. Anybody who wishes to use or operate an Em-Power Disc must become a member of the 'Official Em-Power Research Project'. Each person will receive an exclusive membership number and certificate as a mark of authenticity.

# REPORTED REACTIONS TO THE EM-POWER DISC AND EM-POWER THERAPY

These reactions vary from person to person depending on their physical and emotional state of being. They can range from spontaneous physical movements to very subtle structural adjustments, from profound and emotional releases to just simply feeling better and more confident.

The typical initial reaction to the Em-Power Disc is usually one of extreme scepticism and disbelief. The idea that a piece of purple aluminium can have any of the following reported effects is so difficult for any logical person to accept that most people need to experience it for themselves.

Usually when you hold the Disc, subtle physical and emotional changes take place. Physical changes usually include the spontaneous raising of one or both arms. This may at first, seem a little strange. Many people, if they do not fully understand the concept, usually react by saying something like "this feels really weird!" Lack of understanding leads to a perceived lack of control, and it is this perceived lack of control that can initially frighten some people. Once we understand that we merely have to tell the body to put our arms back down, and that our body will respond immediately, we usually lose any apprehension or misgivings we may have initially felt.

These feelings then usually change into ones of intrigue and excitement. Once we realise that we just have to give a simple command sequence to our body and it will respond in a precise and controlled way, the endless possibilities are overwhelming.

I remember the first time a medical doctor tried the Em-Power Disc. He completely disbelieved the whole concept initially, and told me that he would only try the Disc to prove to me that it was my imagination. I put the Disc in his right hand, his arms raised almost immediately and he responded by dropping the Disc on the floor in disbelief, shouting, "What was that?" When I told him that arm raising was a normal reaction to the Em-Power Disc, he was astounded, and replied "But I don't believe in it". I simply shrugged my shoulders and gave the electricity example again: "When you came into this room, you switched on the light, giving no thought as to whether you believed the light was going to come on or not. In this instance, your belief bore no relevance! There are reasons why the light might not have come on *(a)* that the switch was faulty, *(b)* there could be a break in the cable, *(c)* no electricity supply and *(d)* there was no light bulb in the socket. Providing all four elements of this particular equation exist, then the light will come on".

Another useful example is that of gravity. Our belief in gravity bears no relevance whatsoever. If we throw an apple off a three-storey building, the force of gravity will still squash it as it hits the pavement. After my comments, the doctor wanted to try the Em-Power Disc again. Both his arms raised and he felt the energy flowing through him. He continuously commented on how he was feeling, expressing himself as if nobody had felt that way before! He was still a little tentative at this point, but when I showed him that all he had to say was "Put both my arms back down now" and that his body responded immediately, his mood changed to one of intrigue and inquisitiveness. It took a few moments more for the doctor to fully understand that it was his connection to his Higher Self that had been triggered. That *he* was fully responsible for, and in control of, his body movements, and that it wasn't some 'external' force trying to control him. Once this eventually sank in, he became very relaxed and excited about it.

I then showed him some very basic ways for him to talk to his Higher Self through the body, like "Make me feel very happy now". He immediately responded to this particular command by laughing hysterically. After this very limited trial he reacted in the same way as most other people, insisting that he wanted to know more about the scientific aspects of it, such as how it works and how I made them.

I then illustrated the medical and psychological potential of Em-Power Therapy by showing him how he could use his Higher Self to relieve and self-rectify his back problem. Instantly, he received relief to his back. He was very impressed after this and he thought it was amazing. I explained that I hadn't shown him more than two or three percent of what we already knew about the potential and use of the Em-Power Disc. He then asked me if I thought it would be appropriate for him to try it on some of his patients in those extreme cases where conventional medicine seemed to have had no benefits.

On another occasion, I met with an experienced hypnotherapist who understood the workings of the subconscious mind and thought that the Em-Power Disc was merely a self-hypnotic technique. In response to her enquiry, I simply thought that she should try it and make up her own mind. As usual I placed the Disc in her hand and she immediately felt a warm buzzing feeling coming from it. Then an overwhelming sense of euphoria enveloped her and absorbed her entire body. I took her through the basic steps and she responded in a similar way to that of the doctor.

We have previously stated that hypnotherapy works on the premise that the subconscious mind is like a six-year-old child that stores experiences as memories, emotions and sensory information. Normally when a hypnotherapist is communicating with a person's subconscious mind, the person is placed in an extreme state of relaxation. It is within this state of 'altered' perception that the hypnotherapist is able to use repetitive suggestions upon which the subconscious mind is persuaded to take on-board new concepts and ideas that may be beneficial. The important point in hypnotherapy is the use of repetitive suggestion.

The Em-Power Disc and the communication method used does not respond or work in a similar way. In fact, the Higher Self views repetitive suggestions in an almost insulting manner. The Higher Self is an intelligent force; far beyond our normal perceived intellect and certainly not like a six-year-old child. In actual fact, if a command sequence is repeated more than three times within a specific time frame, then the Higher Self may ignore the instruction altogether. The result in this case would be no reaction, or a withdrawal of a previous reaction.

# VARIOUS REACTIONS
# TO THE EM-POWER DISC

*Mild tingling sensations in the body*
*Hot and cold feelings on a physical level*
*Emotional releases - from bursts of tears and crying, to states of euphoria and extreme happiness, manifesting in laughter*
*Internal manipulations*
*Spontaneous exercise routines. These often take the form of oriental or Eastern energy releasing dances, such as Tai Chi, Qigong, Yoga and others*
*Short periods of mild dizzy spells*
*Internal changes, the release of energy blockages*
*The correction of physical problems*
*Spontaneous arm movements that manipulate your body - either massage, gentle tapping, pinching or rubbing*
*Some people have reported out of body experiences*
*Resolution of suppressed childhood experiences, through visualisation*
*Some people can feel a mild nausea at first, especially in the solar plexus area. This is usually associated with emotional or spiritual blockages or issues that need resolving, and the feelings will pass*
*Unusual and vivid dreams that are controllable, lucid and insightful - resolving issues within the subconscious mind in a state of relaxation through our dreams, rather than having to go through the experience in a conscious state*
*Various states of consciousness from extreme clarity of mind in order to make proper decisions, to a dream like state similar to that of hypnosis.*

Often there can be a combination of any of these reactions, depending on the person's individual physical state and emotional condition. The physical feelings will disappear once the blockages have been removed or the issues have been resolved.

Any feeling or experience you may have, however unusual you may consider it to be, has more than likely been experienced by someone else using the Em-Power Disc. Regardless of the varied reactions, most of these responses only occur while positive changes are taking place. Therefore we consider all responses to be of benefit as they are part of the process. The most important point to remember is that these experiences resolve problems and issues and inevitably have a long lasting, positive effect on a person's well-being.

# THE EM-POWER RESEARCH PROJECT

## What is the Em-Power Research Project?

<>      The ongoing study of how we can transform the information, concepts and ideas contained within this book from theory into practical reality.

## Who is the Em-Power Research Project for?

<>      It is for anyone who wants to achieve better health on all levels and who would like to know and understand more positive and practical ways in which they can fulfil their true potential.

<>      It is for anyone who believes that they are 'more' than merely a physical body.

<>      It is for anyone who has any kind of physical, emotional or spiritual problem.

<>      It is for anyone who would like to enhance or improve their own natural healing abilities.

<>      It is for anyone who would like to instigate positive physical, emotional and spiritual changes.

<>      It is for anyone who would like full and total control over their own lives.

<>      It is for anyone who is prepared to take responsibility for their own self-healing and personal development.

<>      It is for anyone who wants to succeed in relationships, develop new friends, learn how to use new and exciting abilities and also learn how to improve, enhance and optimise existing 'gifts'.

<>      It is for anyone who would like to help members of their family and friends.

<>      It is for anyone who would like to find their 'inner knowledge' and uncover the 'truth'.

<>      It is for all those who are afraid of making changes.

<>      It is for anyone who would like a system of communication that is 'non-religious' and that doesn't include faith or belief, in order for it to work.

## How is Em-Power Therapy unique from all other therapies?

<>      The Em-Power Disc is the only interactive communication method that we know of that allows the 'user' to talk to and instruct the body and mind. Using Em-Power Therapy we receive spontaneous results on a physical, emotional and spiritual level, with no conscious effort but with complete conscious control. Using verbal command sequences, we can achieve such a lot with so little effort in such a short space of time.

It is also the first system in the world to use 'interactive coded fields'. The information is stored within aluminium, so that the energy field of the body can read it. The Em-Power Disc is unique as it acts as a trigger to enable you to ask your Higher Self questions and receive answers and advice in return, to help guide you. All responses, answers, advice and guidance come directly from the Higher Self of the user. Em-Power Therapy can provide the proof that we need to illustrate that we are all much more than a 'physical' body. This can often remove any inherent fears over death and the 'unknown'.

Everyone possesses incredible abilities on some level. Em-Power Therapy demonstrates and teaches us ways in which we can tap into and use them positively, for the benefit of ourselves and others.

## Why is it important to use Em-Power Therapy now?

<>      In the world today there are increasing pressures on people to succeed financially and materially. There is a focus on performance and we have a tendency to judge both ourselves and others, not by who we are but by 'what' we have accomplished on a material level. The faster we can realise and understand our true potential then the easier and happier our lives will be. No matter how good we think we are, we can always be better. In our everyday lives we need to find different ways of dealing with situations, expand our awareness and apply ourselves, turning negative energy into positive energy. Practical application of Em-Power Therapy gives a person the ability to live their life to the full, shed their worries and fears and achieve their goals much faster.

The more healthy a person is on an emotional, physical and spiritual level, the longer their life span and the greater their own development will be. If we want to change our experiences of our external world, then positive changes in our inner perception must take place first.

In the past, when Em-Power Therapy was in its early stages, it was literally a 'last resort' for some people who suffered severe physical and emotional problems. Many had tried other alternative therapies as well as conventional medicine beforehand. Due to our consistent results, more and more people are finding that Em-Power Therapy can improve their lives. Today, healthy individuals, including doctors and therapists and top international athletes use Em-Power Therapy. It is important to understand that Em-Power Therapy is not just for those who are ill. Everyone can gain from using this system.

*Over the past three years we have received many, many letters from people all over the world who have tried Em-Power Therapy and are using the Em-Power Disc. Here are just some of their comments:*

"I am intrigued at the sensations I experienced. I felt tingling sensations, very hot hands and I seem to smile all the time, generally feeling happy in myself and enthusiastic...

I have just done the 'unblocking your chakras' exercise. It's great, and didn't take that long! The sensations were lovely - little shudders here and there...

When I cleansed my Aura it was amazing - I felt a real coolness surrounding me, like a light breeze, really lovely!"

*C. K. / Western Australia*

"Having lived with the pain and discomfort for so long with my frozen shoulder, I had forgotten what it was like to be pain free and enjoy the freedom of movement we all take for granted".

*D. N./Altrincham*

"I have been meditating for 20 years and have accomplished more in one week with the Disc than in all that time...

The negative chatter-box in my head seems to have been replaced by a quite peaceful stillness...."

*C. T./Liverpool*

"My head moved from side to side, my leg started bending and I began to shake and then the pain went".

*H. B./ Manchester (muscular back pain for 10 years)*

"I felt a tingling sensation and the pain disappeared completely, I have full movement in my thumb. All the pressure has lifted and I feel 100%".

*J. M./Rochdale (frozen shoulder for 15 years, severed median nerve and tendons in hand for 18 years)*

"After the pain had gone in my shoulders I still could not accept it and it took me a whole day to come to terms with the idea. The next day I realised it was not my imagination. My shoulders were completely straight".

*W. O./ Manchester (dislocated shoulder, intense pain and mis-alignment due to a bad fall)*

"I felt warmth, relaxation, pins and needles, and a pulling pain. Very exciting, very pleased, quite an unbelievable and enjoyable experience. I never would have believed it. My leg straightened, I can put my foot on the floor, I have no back pain and the pain in my ribs has gone!"

*H. C./Lancs (curved spine for 14 years)*

"I have had very bad pain for 7 years and have to take strong pain-killers. When I tried the Disc my body became straight I became pain free! I can't believe this! I'd forgotten what it felt like to be pain-free. How does one explain this phenomenon, I am sitting on a chair for the first time in weeks. Tomorrow I look forward to putting on my socks".

*S. N./ Manchester (extreme pain in back due to curved spine for 7 years)*

"My lower back began to twist on its own and over the next 5 minutes 90% of the pain disappeared. All I can say is it's a miracle!"

*A. B. / Lancs (trapped nerve in neck and lower back)*

"There were spontaneous body movements into twisted stances. I had a feeling of being around (not outside) my body. Now I'm doing spontaneous muscle-tightening movements and have improved my body shape and posture. My condition now is much calmer, and I have improved digestion.

"I'm 47 and have spent a lot of money, time and energy on all kinds of health 'cures'. The worst thing was the disappointment when they didn't work. This was worth my last try! Interestingly I cut my hand gardening yesterday and 'commanded' it to stop bleeding - it did! This is good because it require no beliefs, self denial, diets, discipline or huge payments".

*Mrs S./Cheshire (suffered arthritis mainly in hips, knees and hand area for 17 years. Autoimmune problems, ME, Dry Eye, Eczema, panic attacks. Previously tried hypnosis, homeopathy, naturopath, vitamins, Ayur Veda)*

"I can walk much better, I feel I could walk for miles! During the process I felt very relaxed and confident, now I feel 10 years younger..."

*C. A./Lancs (hip, knee and neck problems, arthritis)*

"My shoulders were in alignment following treatment, whereas before they were not in a straight line".

*B. B./Bury, Lancs (shoulder/disc out of alignment for 17 years)*

"When I first tried the Em-Power Disc I was somewhat intrigued and mystified by my own body's reactions on an involuntary basis. I was amazed! Now I feel much, much better. I have used it nearly every day since I joined the research programme in mid March '97. I use it for stress-relief, arthritis, energy boosting and daily confidence and self-assertion as well as body corrections. A few minutes a day seems to work wonders".

*P. B./Cheshire (diagnosed with osteoarthritis in the neck)*

"I found it a very strange experience, one that sounded fantastical, verging on a con, but nonetheless it quite clearly worked in some way. I thought initially that it might be hypnosis, but once I tried it out I realised that it didn't seem to be the whole story. I could feel my energy moving through me, it felt right! I am fascinated and impressed. It's like a moving meditation".

*S. B./London*

"I felt really relaxed, at ease. I have much less pain now and feel more comfortable".

*K. C./Cheshire (slipped disc, severe pain)*

"My initial response to the idea was 'unbelievable'. I felt good when I tried the Em-Power Disc. It was working on my shoulder and people standing around me could see my shoulder go back. It also worked on my lower back problem. I feel overall much more confident since I started using Em-Power Therapy. Everyone has noticed a change in me!"

C. C./London (lower back disc problems, suffered from severe pain).

"So far I have achieved some good results from the Em-Power Disc. This has been a very difficult time in my life and the disc has helped me considerably. I also find it useful in meditation. Thank you for this remarkable gift..."

L. C./Merseyside

"I was willing to try anything to get rid of the pain, after years of suffering. This seems to have worked. I now feel 100% better and I think Em-Power Therapy is fantastic. I am now pain free and feeling good".

C. D./Lancs (extreme pain, heart by-pass 6 years)

"At first I was unsure what to expect. I felt a tingling in my arms and down my hands, which faded out. I felt warmth throughout and a movement in my back. I was much happier inside. I had pain in my shoulders but I'm OK now".

G. E./Lancs (spinal muscular atrophy)

"Before the pain went away I felt very emotional and started to cry. I had to sit down and my hands and legs kept moving. I felt happy after that. I would most definitely recommend this to anyone".

J. E./Cheshire (arthritis in both knees, quite severe pain for 2 years)

"The Em-Power Disc gave me immediate and noticeable results. What more do you need?!"

J. F./Lancs (muscular problems)

"I had an accident as a child which was not treated properly. The pain has got worse as I've got older and it's been strong for about 40 years now. I had an open mind when I was introduced to the Em-Power Disc, and found it very interesting. I now feel as if I have benefited from the healing, it feels more physical than other healing methods".

L. F./Manchester

"I felt that this had got to be worth trying. The world needs something like this...."

D. F./Devon

"I had tried spiritual healing before, but I felt wonderful when I first tried the Em-Power Disc. Afterwards, I felt more confident in myself and was able to cope better with things. It would be good if everyone knew about this.

"I don't know why but I seem to be eating a lot healthier, I'm not longing for chocolate and cakes all the time and I have lost weight, which I am really pleased with. The Em-Power Disc is certainly magical. I have had both healing and 'spontaneous writing' since last Sunday".

W. H./Surrey (migraine and headaches)

"I went from initial scepticism to sheer amazement watching the effect on other people. Then to experience it myself, it felt incredible.

"On a subtle level I feel as though it has made a difference to my life. I have more inner confidence, especially at work. I feel more creative and more buoyant about the future".

*J. H./Cheshire (history of back problems)*

"My spine is still curved, but my shoulders have gone back and there is a noticeable change in my posture after only one session".

*B. K./Lancs (curvature of the spine)*

"The Em-Power Disc is easy to use. It works and you can do it yourself!"

*G. M./North Wales*

"When I tried the Disc it was as if my awareness extended beyond my physical self. It is the most powerful thing I have ever encountered. It puts you in touch with the universal consciousness, which will teach, guide and help you become the best you can be. It helped me stop smoking, but this connection will help with anything you ask for. I now feel wonderful, empowered. I am changed forever".

*S. M./Kings Lynn*

"When I heard about the Disc I was willing to try it, I kept an open mind and just hoped that it would work. I was amazed that it did..."

*S.M./ Berkshire*

"I feel elated because I can use it for myself - the possibilities are endless..."

*K. M./Lancs*

"I have had consistent pain for 16 years due to shoulder dislocation and hip and back problems, as a result of a car accident. When I tried the Em-Power Disc a feeling of warmth overcame me. Then slow, twisting sensations started at the top half of my body, but my lower half didn't move. I am amazed at the results of this session".

*K. N./Manchester (dislocated shoulder and back problems)*

"I broke my knee and ankle in a car crash 5 years ago and it's still very painful. I got an instantaneous response from the Disc and I use it every day. I now feel 100% better and would recommend this experience to others".

*C. O./Durham*

"I find Em-Power Therapy a fascinating subject and I intend to learn as much about it as possible. It's all very exciting, at first I was apprehensive, but that soon gave way to elation".

*M. P./Surrey (Hip, lower back and groin problems)*

"I have pain and poor posture due to an arm fracture. I tried other alternative treatments such as aurosoma and homeopathy before using the Disc. Now I feel 90% better. The pain has considerably reduced in my arm and the first time I activated the Disc my posture corrected automatically. It now gives me arm stretching exercise and I think that the bone is in a better position for healing".

*K. R./Cheshire*

"I had a nervous breakdown 5 years ago which still affects me. The Em-Power Disc is a priceless piece of metal! It felt so good to tap into the

ancient and knowing part of myself. It's powerful stuff. Now I feel much more in control of myself and my destiny".
*H. S./Devon*

"I have extreme pain 24 hours a day and it's been like that for 5 years. I didn't know what to expect when I tried the Em-Power Disc I experienced hot sensations throughout my body and then the pain went away. I feel that it is a wonderful alternative cure!"
*J. S./Manchester*

"For 3 years I have had a high level of constant pain. After my treatment I had a feeling of well being and confidence. At one point, an emotional tide of feelings washed over me. I would say that my pain after one session is 80% better".
*A. S./Manchester (diagnosed with degenerate disease of the spine)*

"Dear Coby, Just wanted to let you know how much more positive and safer I'm feeling - thanks for everything".
*K. S./Manchester*

"I have had ME since 1987 and fractured my spine after a serious car accident, causing me immobility and severe pain. I think that the Em-Power Healing System is a unique method of healing, which is all encompassing. Most other therapies only touch on the symptoms. I have had no physical reaction, I don't move at all, as yet. But I've had brilliant results with insomnia".
*P. S./N.Ireland*

"This is just what the world needs!"
*Mrs M.T./Manchester*

"By putting my Em-Power Disc on my neck where the pain was the most severe, it made my neck very hot at first. I had a good night's sleep, the best for over a week. I've done this a couple of times since and my neck is 95% better. I do the same thing for my headaches, I put the Disc at the point of pain and after a few moments it just disappears. My smoking habit has greatly reduced and the good thing is that I now know that I can stop if I really want to. I have asked for an exercise for my back problem and it moves me from side to side, bends my knees and from there I have to lie on the floor, rolling and stretching. My legs move and then go straight up in the air and when this happens there is a 'pushing up' sensation".
*Mrs J.W./Surrey*

"This is a most fascinating treatment. I am amazed at how the pain just disappeared".
*M. Y./Manchester (experienced severe pain after an operation 6 years ago)*

## INDEX/GLOSSARY

152

*Continued...*

---

IF YOU WOULD LIKE MORE INFORMATION REGARDING THE
EM-POWER RESEARCH PROJECT AND HOW YOU CAN
OBTAIN AN EM-POWER DISC OF YOUR OWN, THEN PLEASE
CONTACT:

**ZVIKLER HEALING RESEARCH UK LTD
PO BOX 90
PRESTWICH
MANCHESTER
M45 6ZH**
Tel/Fax:  0161 773 1731
e-mail: heatherpedley@compuserve.com
website: www.empower-disc.co.uk